THE
DIAMOND
SWORD

THE
DIAMOND
SWORD

REDISCOVERING MEDITATION
The forgotten treasure of India

OSHO

JAICO PUBLISHING HOUSE

Ahmedabad Bangalore Bhopal Bhubaneswar Chennai
Delhi Hyderabad Kolkata Lucknow Mumbai

Published by Jaico Publishing House
A-2 Jash Chambers, 7-A Sir Phirozshah Mehta Road
Fort, Mumbai - 400 001
jaicopub@jaicobooks.com
www.jaicobooks.com

THE DIAMOND SWORD
ISBN 978-81-8495-448-7

First Jaico Impression: 2013

The material in this book is from the original series of
OSHO Talks, *Koplen Phir Phoot Aayeen* and *Phir Amrit Ki Bund Pari*,
given to a live audience. The complete OSHO text
archive can be found via the online OSHO Library at
www.osho.com

Printed by
B.B. Press
A-37, Sector - 67
Noida - 201301, U.P.

CONTENTS

Miseries are not clinging to you, remember – you are clinging to your miseries.

You can drop your miseries only when some inner meaning starts flowering in you. Miseries can be dropped only when meditation starts blooming in you because then you start enjoying your emptiness, it is no longer empty. Emptiness itself starts having a positive fragrance; it isn't negative anymore.

That's the whole magic of meditation: it transforms your emptiness into a positive fulfillment, into something overwhelming. Emptiness becomes silence, emptiness becomes peace, and emptiness becomes divine, it becomes godliness.

There is no greater magic than meditation. To transform the negative into the positive, to transform darkness into light, that is the miracle of meditation. To transform a trembling person into a fearless soul, to transform a person who was clinging to every stupid thing into a nonclinger, into a nonpossessor, that is what happens through meditation.

Buddha used to call meditation a great sword, it cuts your problems at the very root. It makes you aware that you need not be afraid of your inner abyss. It is beautiful, it is blissful. You have not experienced its bliss and beauty because you have never gone into it, you have always been escaping. You have not tasted of it; it is nectar, it is not poison. But how are you going to know without tasting it? You are running away from something which can become your life's fulfillment. You are running away from something which is the only thing worth achieving. You are running away from yourself.

Osho

The Dhammapada: The Way of the Buddha, Volume 12

CHAPTER 1

Osho,
How are you?

I am the same…and you, also, are the same. That which changes is not our real face, is not our soul. That which does not change – neither in life nor in death – that alone is our reality. We ask people, "How are you?" We shouldn't, because in the very asking we have embraced the transitory: childhood, youth, old age, birth, death.

You know that there is something within you which was the same in childhood and was the same even when you were not yet born. So much water has flowed down the Ganges, but you are standing on the bank and you are still the same. Tomorrow you will be seen no more…then, too, you will be the same. Forms will be new, shapes will be new – perhaps you may not even recognize yourself. Names will be new, identities will be new, your clothes will be new, and yet I say, *you* will be the same. You have always been the same, and you will be the same forever. If you like you can call this eternal, everlasting ancient-ness "godliness," or if you want you can call this your *is-ness* – many waves coming and going, but the ocean remaining the same.

Change is a lie, but we have accepted change as the reality and have made it our world. If we could only understand that change is a lie, then there would remain no difference between a thief and a saint – because that which is within both of them is neither thief nor saint. Then, there will remain no difference between a Hindu and a Mohammedan – their languages may be different, but hidden under their languages is an entity called the witness. Their actions may be different, but hidden behind their actions is something which is forever the same. And it is the search for that which is eternal which is called religion.

In fact, people should be asking each other, "Hopefully...you haven't changed?" However this world is upside-down and its ways are upside-down, and its behaviors are all nonsensical. But because the crowd follows them, everyone else also complies.

When you look at your face in the mirror you think you have seen yourself. I wish it were that easy – then everyone would be self-realized. When you hear your name, you think you know your name. If it were so cheap, there would be no need for religion in the world. Your name is not yours; it is borrowed and stale. You came into the world without a name and you will go from the world without a name.

When we are carrying a dead body to the crematorium, we chant: "*Ram naam satya hai*" – the name of Rama is the truth. Strange that nobody mentions the dead man's name – although that was his truth his whole life, and now, suddenly, it is thrown away. When the man was born, he came without a name; now when he is dying suddenly Rama's name becomes the truth and his own becomes a lie....

No, Rama's name – the eternal truth – *is* the truth throughout life. And every hour, each moment, man is on the funeral pyre. Any moment your journey toward the crematorium can begin.

There is a saying: "Ask not for whom the bell tolls." When someone dies, the church bells toll to inform the whole village. So, the saying is: "Ask not for whom the bell tolls, it tolls for thee" – no matter who has died. It is always your own funeral procession even though you yourself may be attending at the graveside. The corpse burning on the funeral pyre is always your corpse, even if you yourself have set it alight.

The greatest dilemma of life is that we have taken that which is forever changing to be the reality and have completely forgotten about that which is unchanging.

I am the same. There is simply no way to be anything other than what we are. Even if one wants to, one cannot be anything other than what one is. For your whole life you are trying to become something. All your ambitions, all your hurrying and scurrying is only

3

so you can somehow be something else. And what is the misfortune of life? – that no one ever succeeds in becoming something else. And the biggest surprise is that you have always been that which you are, you always were: no matter how much you have run around, how fast you have raced, you still remained the same. But even up until the last moment of their lives people don't realize this.

The day that you become aware that "I don't have to become anything, I only have to discover that which I already am," on that day the moment of revolution has arrived in your life; the moment of godliness has arrived in your life. You have arrived at the temple door. Now, you cannot be burned on the funeral pyre; now, your name cannot be changed. Now, centuries will come and go, stars will rise and fall, but your being has touched that spot where all is unmoving, all is calm, all is silent; where there is no commotion, no stirring, no wave. This unstirred music is called *samadhi*, the attainment of self-realization. To become this void is to become the truth.

People come to me to become something. And my difficulty is that I want to demolish them so that they remain only that which they really are – *that* is the gift of the existence. And all that we build for ourselves are children's castles made of sand – a tiny gust of wind and they will all collapse – or lines drawn on water which begin to disappear even before they are drawn. But you go on building these sand castles; you don't even look back to see that all that you build disappears, is lost.

And it is not just this one time, but a thousand times; it is not only in this life, but in thousands of lives, that you have been doing the same thing. For how long will you go on doing the same things? One may err once – that is forgivable – but the second time it becomes unforgivable. And yet we are making the same mistakes thousands of times. Now, the only thing we know is how to commit mistakes. Now, the only thing we know is how to keep going round and round in that circle of mistakes – and so many mistakes, and such a crowd of mistakes that what gets lost in it was actually your real being.

From the day I recognized myself I have not come across any change within me. Everything has changed, every day it will go on changing, but someone deep within, standing quietly – in health, in sickness, in success, in failure – is exactly the same.

I came to experience many things in the American jails that perhaps would never have happened outside, because I was dragged around through five jails without any reason, without any crime. But perhaps I am wrong: what I don't consider to be criminal, they do. Thinking is a crime, to be peaceful is a crime, to be silent is a crime, meditation is crime. Truth, is perhaps, the greatest sin in this world. For this alone they were punishing me. But their difficulty was – and every jailer told me this at the time of my leaving their prison – "Thousands of prisoners have passed through my jail, but the one thing about you that gives me sleepless nights is that we are trying to harass you and you are enjoying the whole thing!"

I would say to them, "It is beyond your understanding, because the one you are harassing is not me. I am the one that is enjoying the whole thing."

And when the journalists outside the jails would ask me, "How are you?" and I would reply, "I am exactly the same as ever before." It would be beyond the wits of an American journalist. He would say, "Don't you don't feel any difference between being in jail and being out of jail?"

I would say, "There is tremendous difference between being inside the jail and outside the jail, but you have asked something else. You have asked about me – not about the jail. Inside the jail or outside the jail – I am the same. The inside of the jail is different, the outside of the jail is different; I am the same even in my handcuffs, and I will be the same when I am free of the handcuffs. How can handcuffs change me or the prison walls change me?"

At the time of leaving the last prison, the head of that prison said to me, "This is the most unique experience of my whole life. I have seen people happy before coming into the jail, but I had never seen anyone still happy by the time they were leaving the jail. You are leaving the same as you came in. What is the secret?"

I said, "That itself is exactly my crime – that I was teaching people this very secret." Your government, and no other government in the world, wants people to understand this secret, because the moment people understand this secret, all the power governments have over you will disappear. Jails will become useless, guns will become meaningless, unused cartridges will become like used cartridges; no fire will be able to burn you nor will any sword be able to cut you. That is why those who are sitting on your chest through the power of the sword and of fire never want you to recognize who you really are – because that will destroy their whole power. Your recognition of yourself is their death. And it is not surprising that over the centuries whenever someone has tried to remind you of yourself, the governments, the vested interests, have come in the way.

The crime that Socrates was charged with before being poisoned was that he was teaching people to be immoral. He was only teaching people to know who they were. But the peddlers of morality felt that if people come to know who they are, "what will happen to our trade?"

So never ask anyone: "How are you?" Only ask, "Have you come to recognize the changeless?" The number of such people who know the changeless should increase in this world. They alone are the salt of the earth. They alone are the essence. Only their existence is meaningful.

Only those who have known existence have become free of their debt to existence.

Osho,
You say that religiousness flowers only in the East and people
from the West come to India in search of religiousness.
Then why didn't those same countries welcome you?
Why did they insult you like this?

Because of you. At least, they didn't try to kill me by throwing a knife at me; in India you did. They didn't try to disturb my meetings by throwing stones; in India you did. And when one's very own cannot understand, then to expect that much from others is not right.

For the past two thousand years you have been in slavery. Your slavery and poverty has given the West the idea that you are worthless, that you are not even alive – you are a community of dead people.

And those who went to the West before me – Vivekananda, Ramateertha, Yogananda and other Hindu sannyasins – none of them were insulted in the West; no doors were closed for them, because they resorted to lies. They compared Jesus with Buddha; they compared the Bible with the Upanishads and the Gita. They glorified Western people even further. You were slaves, you were poor; your sannyasins proved you to be even spiritually poor. They diminished your spiritual heights and placed them alongside the ordinary valleys of the West.

My situation was altogether different. I told the West that India is only poor now – it has not always been so. There was a day when India was called a golden bird. And the heights that India has touched in the past, you have never even dreamed about. And what you call religion cannot even be called that in the face of the heights India once reached. Jesus is a non-vegetarian and he drinks. No religion of India can accept this, that its highest expression of mankind is non-vegetarian and drinks wine – that he doesn't even have this much compassion, that he destroys life for his own food; that he disrespects life so much for his own food! And a person who drinks wine…there is not even a question of him attaining the heights of meditation. Sad people drink alcohol, disturbed and tense people drink alcohol – because the characteristic of alcohol is to make you oblivious of the state you are in. If you are sad, disturbed, unhappy, you forget it for a while by drinking wine. Next day, all your unhappiness is back again. Alcohol does not destroy unhappiness; it only makes you forget it. Meditation destroys unhappiness; it does not merely make you forget it. Meditation and alcohol are opposites. In Christianity, there is no place for meditation anywhere.

But your Vivekananda and Yogananda and Ramateertha, just in order to obtain praise from the West, remained busy explaining that Jesus belongs to the same category as Buddha belongs to, as Mahavira belongs to. This was a lie. And because I said only what was truthful,

7

naturally door after door went on closing against me. I do not accept that there are any such heights in the statements of Jesus as can be found in the Upanishads, or there is anything as special in his life as there is in the life of Buddha. His "specialties" are ordinary. Even if a person can walk on water, he is, at the most, a magician. And in any case, the only mention of him ever walking on water is in the Christian books themselves.

If Jesus did walk on water, what is spiritual in it? Firstly, he didn't walk. And if he did, the pope should demonstrate the ability, if nowhere else then at least in a swimming pool. Forget the swimming pool, how about in a bathtub? Even that much evidence will be sufficient, because the pope is the representative – and an infallible one. He never commits a mistake. And even if somebody *has* walked on water, what has that got to do with spirituality?

A man came to Ramakrishna. He was an old yogi, he was older than Ramakrishna. Ramakrishna was sitting on the bank of the Ganges and this man came and said, "I have heard that people worship you. But if you really have any spirituality in your life, come and walk on the Ganges with me."

Ramakrishna said, "You must be tired from the journey. Just sit down and relax a bit – we can walk on the Ganges later. Right now, I am not meant to be going anywhere either; and in the meanwhile we could get familiar with one another. We do not know each other. And by the way, how much time did you spend in learning to walk on water?"

The man said, "Eighteen years."

Ramakrishna started laughing. He said, "I have never walked on water, because I cross the Ganges for just two paise. To me, wasting eighteen years learning a task that is accomplished by just two paise is foolishness, not spirituality. And what is spiritual in being able to walk on water? What mystery of life have you unraveled through it?

I remember an incident that will explain the difference to you.

It is said of Jesus that he called a dead person back to life. It is something worth considering that people are dying every day, and he resurrected only one dead person back to life! It is a little surprising that someone who could bring the dead back to life did so only to one person – and that person, too, his own friend, Lazarus. The whole thing is a made-up story.

Lazarus is lying in a cave, Jesus comes and calls out: "Lazarus, wake up! Come from death back to life." And Lazarus immediately comes out of the cave.

Now many things are worth considering here.

The first thing: this man is a childhood friend of Jesus. The second thing: a man who has returned back from death to life...there should be a revolution in his life. No revolution took place in the life of Lazarus. Other than this incident, there is no mention of Lazarus anywhere else. Do you think that a man returning from the realm of death, having seen what is beyond death, will remain the same? And if Jesus could save one man, there was no need for anyone in Judea to die.

I am taking up this incident because a similar incident happened in Gautam Buddha's life.

Gautam Buddha arrived in a village and the only son of a widow had just died. The woman was living only for this son of hers. You can imagine her situation: she almost went mad.

The people of the village said to her, "Going mad won't help at all. Gautam Buddha has arrived in the village. Bring the dead body of your son into his presence and say to him, 'You are an enlightened being, please bring my son back to life. I have lost everything. The only hope in my life was this son and now I have lost him too. Now there is nothing else left in my life.'"

Buddha said to that woman, "Certainly I will bring your son back to life by the evening, but before that you will have to fulfill one condition. Go back to your village and bring some mustard seeds from a house in which no one has ever died. Bring those seeds and I will revive your son."

That mad woman – she was naturally almost in a state of madness – rushed away. She went to this house, to that house, and people said to her, "You are asking for merely a handful of mustard seeds, whereas

9

we would be only too happy to pile up bullock-cart loads of mustard seeds in order to bring your son back to life. But the problem is our seeds wouldn't help – in our houses so many people have died!"

By the evening she had received the same answer from every house in the village: "Our seeds won't help. This is a very paradoxical condition that Buddha has given you, Where is there a home in which no one has ever died?"

This day-long encounter with the truth became a revolution in that woman's life. She came back, fell at Gautam Buddha's feet and said, "Please, forget everything, forget that my son has died. Everyone here has to die. You gave me the right teaching. Now please help me so that I can know who or what it is that lives within me as life. Please, initiate me as a seeker of the truth."

This woman who had come begging for her son's life now stood in front of Buddha praying to him to help her discover her own life. She became a sannyasin, and she became one of Gautam Buddha's foremost disciples who attained to the ultimate state called enlightenment.

This I call revolution.

Even if Buddha had brought her dead son back to life, so what? One day he was going to die again. Lazarus, too, must have died again one day. But Buddha used the situation to give it a new dimension, a spiritual perspective.

In the East, we are not used to looking at everything from the outer, the superficial level. I see that what Buddha did is great and what Jesus did is very ordinary, it has no value.

My statements made the West alarmed. The reason for this was that the West has become accustomed to one thing: that the East is poor. Send missionaries there and convert the poor into Christians! And tens of millions of people are converting to Christianity. But all these people in the East who are converting to Christianity are poor, orphaned, tribal, starving and unclothed. They have nothing to do with religion; all they want are schools, hospitals, medicine, clothing, food and education for their children. Christianity is buying their religion with bread and butter.

The reason for seeing me as an enemy was that I was not attracting the poor or the orphans or the beggars. And there is no dearth of beggars there: in America alone there are thirty million beggars. Those who are busy converting other beggars in the world into Christianity are not doing anything for their own beggars, because they are already Christians anyway.

The people influenced by me were professors, writers, poets, painters, sculptors, scientists, architects – all intelligent people. And this was a matter of alarm: if the intelligent people of the country are being influenced by this man, it indicates a great danger, because it is these people who decide the course of direction for others too. Seeing them, people walk on those same paths; their footprints will lead others, too, on these very same paths.

And I had never asked anybody to leave their religion. I never asked anybody to accept a new religion. All I said was try to understand for yourself – what religion is and what irreligion is. Then, it is up to you. You are intelligent and rational.

My only crime is that I created this urge in those countries that the East – where you are sending thousands of missionaries to convert people to Christianity – has touched such celestial heights and you are not yet worthy to even crawl on the earth. Your Bible, your prophets, your messiahs, prove to be very childish, very poor and immature in the face of those heights. And this created a fear, a restlessness.

The West has no answer for even a single point of mine. I was ready to discuss it with President Ronald Reagan in the White House, in an open forum, because he is a fundamentalist Christian. He believes that Christianity is the only religion; all other religions are hollow. I sent messages to the pope many times, that "I am ready to come to the Vatican and I want to discuss your religion, in the midst of your own people. And I want to make you aware that what you call religion is not religion, and that you have no idea what religion is." Naturally, I appeared as an enemy to them.

No single individual has ever succeeded in creating so many enemies on such a large scale around the whole world. Parliaments in every country have decided that I cannot enter their countries because

11

I am a dangerous man and I will destroy their morality, their religion.

If a tourist for two weeks can destroy your religion of two thousand years of hard work, then it is not worth saving. Let it be destroyed.

CHAPTER 2

THE
SWORD
OF MEDITATION

Osho,
What to say of the governments and the religions…the idiocy
that even the intelligentsia is displaying in misunderstanding
you is frightening. How can mankind misbehave in this way
with its own highest flower? Is its soul dead? Isn't the ugly
behavior that has been meted out to you over the last ten months
a kind of apartheid on an international level that is even worse
than the apartheid in South Africa?
Would you please like to say something about this?

One thing that I have experienced very deeply in these ten months is
the false mask that is on every person's face. I used to think that only
some people work in drama companies, but as I see it now it feels
as if every man is hidden behind a false mask. These months were
precious, and necessary, in order to see man as he is – and even to
understand that the very man I have been fighting for my whole life
is not worth fighting for. He is a rotten corpse, a skeleton. His masks
are beautiful; his soul, very ugly.

The way in which many countries from all over the world have
welcomed me, makes several conclusions clear. One, that the affluent
countries of the West who have everything – wealth, science, technology, and every arrangement for mankind's destruction – do not have
a single ray of life. And all this material development has naturally
given them a false notion: that they are not only the masters of the
whole world but of everyone's souls as well.

And the people of the East who were visiting the West –

Vivekananda, Ramateertha, Yogananda, Krishnamurti – have all deceived people. And that deception was double-edged: for the West they have created the fallacy that your messiahs, your prophets, your Bibles, your Korans have the same essential message that is there in the Upanishads of the East, in the words of Lao Tzu and at the feet of the Buddha. In this way they have conveyed a lie to the West. And this lie has helped them: they were not opposed, on the contrary they were respected. And the people in the East were also pleased that Vivekananda is being welcomed – in that way, they too are welcomed. But that welcome was not for you; that welcome was for Vivekananda's lie. A single lie did that two-faceted job.

My crime has been that I have told them the truth exactly as it is. I have told them that neither does the West have any religion nor did it ever have, and that the messiahs and the saviors of the West are not worth a penny – they are not even the dust under Gautam Buddha's feet. Not a fraction of the heights of the Upanishads is there in the religious scriptures of the West. Hence I am unable to rank Christ or Moses or Mohammed or Ezekiel in the same category as Buddha and Lao Tzu, Bodhidharma, Bokoju, Chuang Tzu or Nagarjuna. I am helpless. The difference is so vast that to keep them in one and the same category will be the biggest lie in the world.

The delusion of Christianity – that by converting people into Christians it is taking the whole world onto the path of spirituality – is not only a lie, but is such a fallacy that darkness within the world will go on increasing in the same proportion that Christianity spreads. The reason for the opposition to me was that I couldn't give any respect to Christianity. There was nothing worthy of respect.

So on the one hand, the countries in the West, whether democracies or monarchies, are all Christian and under tremendous pressure from Christianity. And even if their politicians understand what I am saying, in order to remain in power they have to accept what the priests are saying as the truth. The priest has control over the votes; he has control over the masses. In this way, I naturally created enemies in the West.

But the most surprising thing is that because India has been in slavery for two thousand years, it continues to look to the West for everything. Whatsoever is accepted in the West – whether it is right or wrong – becomes accepted in the East. And whatsoever is not accepted in the West – even if it is pure gold – becomes dirt. So because all the countries in the West – the rich countries – were against me, the Indian politicians, even the wretched Indian journalists who live for a penny and are ready to sell their souls for a penny, all started writing against me. They have nothing to do with me; their concern is that the patronage of the West should continue. Outwardly, slavery has gone, but inwardly the desire to remain slaves has not.

I was kept in American jails for twelve days without any reason – without an arrest warrant, without any grounds. But the Indian government could not gather the courage to ask the American government why an Indian citizen, who has done no crime, was being kept in jail, after being arrested without an arrest warrant, forcibly, under the force of guns – and not even allowing him to see or contact his attorney, against all their own rules. The government of India remained silent. India's ambassador remained silent. Those twelve days were of such shame to me: shame that I was born in India – a country that has no self-respect; a country that has no dignity; a country that has no means to give protection to its citizens. And it would have been possible at least to inquire, at least to ask…after all what is the Indian ambassador who sits in America doing? In those twelve days the only thing that kept piercing my heart like a thorn was, "Has India lost all its soul?"

And the day I was released from the jail – because there were no grounds to keep me in custody – a man from the Indian embassy came to see me, saying, "The prime minister of India has asked us to ask you what can we do for you?"

I said, "Perhaps for the past twelve days, the ministers and the prime minister of India were drugged with opium and the Indian ambassador was lying drunk. Today, when I have been released, you have come to ask me 'Of what service can we be to you?' I do not need your services. Yes, if your prime minister ever needs my services, ask me. And it won't be too long before your prime minister needs my services, because what are the qualifications of these worthless people that you have turned into prime ministers? Is it that if your mother gets shot and killed, you become qualified to be a prime minister? What to say of becoming a prime minister, in this way you don't become qualified even for an office clerk's job. Even if both your mother and father get shot and killed, you will still need qualifications to become a peon in an office. This fact in itself is no qualification."

But just to cover up, to show that "we cared..." But the care came when I was already out of the jail.

India has been in slavery for two thousand years. If this slavery had only made India poor that would not have been such a big thing. But this slavery took away from India even the remembrance that there is also an inner affluence, that there is also a dignity of the soul which can neither be weighed against material wealth nor bought with material wealth. Whatever is significant in life...there is no way to buy it with wealth. And the education that three hundred years of British slavery gave to India was less of an education and more of a poison. It filled India's own genius with anti-Indian poison.

Today, you are not even aware of what amazing heights you were soaring to in the days of the Upanishads. Today, you don't even know of the faraway stars that your mystics, Kabir, Nanak, Dadu and Farid, have touched. Today, you are not even aware that Buddha, Mahavira, have attained to the ultimate peak – the Everest of consciousness latent in mankind. We are the heirs to all of this. And to be an heir is no ordinary responsibility. We have to take this inheritance to the whole world, because man in the world has nothing; man is hollow.

Christianity, Islam and Judaism, the three religions that are born outside of India, are not even worth calling religions. Because where there is no place for meditation, there can be no possibility of religion, and in these three religions, there is no place for meditation. This country has sharpened the science of meditation for thousands of years, has made it into a sword. We have something that no one else has.

Opposing me is not opposing me. I am an ordinary man, a man just like you – what can come of opposing me? The European

Parliament has decided that I cannot even land my plane anywhere, on any European airport. One night at 12 o'clock I arrived at London Airport. I wanted to stay there for six hours – even that was not permissible! And next day there was a question about it in England's parliament, when the prime minister of England, Margaret Thatcher, said, "This man is dangerous." I have no nuclear weapon on me. I would have been sleeping for six hours in my airplane at the airport. What danger would that have created for England?

So this was asked in the parliament – that what was the danger? In the name of danger it was said that this man can destroy the morality of the young people, can destroy the religion of the country; that he can destroy the traditions and the past of our race. And wasn't there at least one single fool in that whole parliament who could have asked, "If all this can be accomplished in six hours from inside an airplane parked at the airport, then what have you been doing for the past two thousand years?" If a morality and the religion – whose lessons are being given in the churches, schools, colleges and the universities – can be destroyed in six hours, then they are worth destroying; there is certainly some lie there. It is only the quality of a lie; only a lie can be destroyed in minutes. If you are under the fallacy that two plus two makes five, then any man can destroy that fallacy in moments. It is only a question of clearly showing that two plus two cannot make five.

So certainly lies have been spread and systems of morality have been based on those lies. And in this world, the biggest hurt that comes to man is when his lies are taken away from him – lies which he thought to be truths, and on the basis of which he thought that he has something.

My only crime was that I exactly said what the case is, and said it exactly as it is.

There is information – and not just from one source, but many – that the American president is ready to pay five million rupees if someone is willing to assassinate me. Now this price is a little too much. What, after all, is the value of a human body? The bodies of animals are valuable – shoes can be made out of their skin, toys can be made out of their bones, medicines can be made out of their chemical parts. In this world, man has the most valueless body. It has no price on it. On the contrary, something needs to be spent in order to cremate it or dispose of it in some other way. You can't even keep it in the house.

If a country is ready to spend five million rupees on my assassination, it is not accidental. The fear is tremendous because I challenged President Ronald Reagan, saying that I was ready to come to the White House. He himself is a fanatic Christian. He believes that no other religion except Christianity is religion. And I said, "I challenge you. I am ready to come to your own home, amongst your own people, for a debate with you. If you can convince me, I will become a Christian and if I convince you, you are to become a sannyasin."

Ronald Reagan knows that the fundamentals upon which he calls his Christianity a religion are utterly foolish. Jesus walked on water...even if he did, it has nothing to do with religion. For one, he never did walk on water, but if he had, then his priests – at least the pope – should demonstrate this ability, if nowhere else, then on a swimming pool. A representative should be able to substantiate it to some degree. If a swimming pool seems to be too big, even a bathtub will suffice. Just two steps will prove that walking on water is against the laws of nature. And religion is not against the laws of nature; religion is an evolution beyond the laws of nature, religion supports the laws of nature. The very meaning of religion is that we can manifest that which is hidden in nature.

But it rests on absurd things: that Jesus revives the dead. What will be the outcome even if you do revive the dead? After all, the Lazarus whom Jesus saved finally died again. And when one has to die finally, what difference does it make whether one dies today or tomorrow? What significance does this reviving give to spirituality? And a man who could revive *one* dead person...it is not that only one person died in his country during his lifetime. People die every day. But Lazarus was a childhood friend and this is all straightforward trickery. A man has been hidden in a cave and Jesus comes and calls out, "Lazarus! Arise from the dead!" and Lazarus immediately comes out.

If Lazarus had really died and then returned after visiting the world of deathlessness that lies beyond death, some new genius should have arisen within his life; some light should have shone through his eyes; some magic should have come into his hands and some authority should have entered his words. But no, after this incident one doesn't find any mention of Lazarus anywhere. Even when he died is not known.

Religions don't arise on such rotten stuff, such rotten stories and fabrications. A science of consciousness is needed to found a religion. Jesus himself doesn't know anything about the science of consciousness. That's why on the cross he is waiting for God and the angels to arrive playing on their harps. Flowers will start showering any moment.

But neither did flowers shower, nor did any harps play, nor did any music arise anywhere. The sky remained as empty as it ever had been. And because Jesus' whole thing was based on belief and was not an experience, in the end it collapsed. He stretched it quite far, consoled himself to the last – with the idea that it is a moment of testing. Finally he shouted toward the sky, "Oh God! Have you forsaken me?" Neither has he any experience of the eternal nor any experience of his soul.

Because I tried to expose Christianity for what it is – and as a result a unique revolution took place amongst the youth of the West, the educated class of the West, the geniuses, painters, sculptors, scientists, doctors, professors, poets, actors, dancers; world renowned people started to join the commune – a fear ran through the whole of Christianity. Up until now they had converted people in the East – from Hinduism to Christianity, from Mohammedanism to Christianity – but the people they had converted were either beggars or orphaned children, or tribal people who didn't even know yet how to wear clothes. Utterly uneducated with no concern for religion, all that they wanted was bread – so along with bread they were also fed religion.

But they didn't succeed in converting a single person from the East to Christianity who understands the Upanishads, who follows the footsteps of the Buddha. My success seemed fatal to them. They were converting our beggars into Christianity; I was releasing their geniuses out of the prison of Christianity. This success was intolerable. This success was my crime.

And you are right in asking, "What has happened to the intelligentsia?" But, this is true only of the intelligentsia of India, not of the intelligentsia of the West. In Italy alone, some sixty-five topmost people from the intelligentsia – amongst whom several are Nobel Prize winners, are world renowned actors, poets – have submitted an application to the Italian government saying that to stop me from visiting Italy is to murder democracy.

You may believe in what I say, you may not, but I cannot be deprived of my right to express it. And if I am deprived of this, then you are strangling yourself. I have tried for the past six months to enter Italy, but the pope is bent upon influencing the Italian government not to allow it.

When the pope came to India, I welcomed him and I opposed those people who were throwing stones at him, showing black flags, calling names and asking the pope to leave. This is not Indian, this is not cultured, this is not a way to protest, this is not human. If the pope has come to India, he should receive invitations from many, many places, saying "We want a dialogue; we want to hear what the foundation stones of your religion are and we want to put the foundation stones of our religion before you so that our people can compare, can reflect. Maybe you are right. And we are only for truth: it doesn't matter from whose mouth the truth is spoken."

The Italian government is making excuses every day – that it will decide today, that it will decide tomorrow. But the pope's influence is great, and he is saying that I should not be allowed entry into Italy. And the biggest reason for his interference is this invitation from sixty-five of the most respected people of Italy to me, and my challenge to debate him at the Vatican. It is not about quarreling and fighting: quarrels and fights are for those who are weak, those who are false. If you have truth itself then words alone are enough. One is not required to pick up a sword.

The German intelligentsia has lodged its opposition. The intelligentsia in Holland has pulled its government into court. The intelligentsia in Spain is fighting for me to be allowed to enter Spain. No one has the right to stop me from that. If you do not want to agree with my views, it is not being forced upon you.

India alone is the country where the intelligentsia did not take issue, where the intelligentsia did not ask the government, "Are you our representatives or our enemies?" The Indian intelligentsia remained quiet, because in fact there is simply no intelligentsia in India. Those you call the intelligentsia of India are ready to sell themselves out for just about nothing. They have no self-dignity, they do not have a religion of their own, they do not have an identity of their own. They have forgotten who they are. And in three hundred years, Britain has deluded them in such a way that they have become clerks, they have become schoolmasters, they have become station masters, they have become journalists. But to be one of the intelligentsia is altogether a different matter – one has to have courage to drink poison. Paying a price to have truth is essential. One is required to be a Socrates. These people are not intellectuals.

But when it is regarding me, the situation becomes even more difficult. The difficulty is that the intellectual of India is divided: either he is Hindu or he is Mohammedan or he is Christian or he is Jaina. I am none of these. I am merely a human being – and who is ready to stand for a human being? A Hindu is not interested. The Hindu *shankaracharya* will be happy if I am assassinated. Perhaps they will celebrate that. The Jaina teachers will be happy: good riddance to trouble! The Mohammedan imam will rejoice.

How many *people* are there in this country?

I am reminded...

A man applied for a job. The boss asked, "How long did you work at your previous place?"

The applicant replied, "I worked for two years."

The boss rang up the place where the applicant had said he had worked, and inquired, "How many days did 'so and so' work for you?"

The boss there said, "Two weeks."

The other boss was amazed. He said, "But the man says he worked for you for two years!"

The other man laughed and said, "He had employment for two years...but he only worked for two weeks."

How many intellectuals here have contributed anything intelligent to the world? And they have a real difficulty with me because they are all chained to their prisons; they have their chains. And I am against their chains as much as I am against the chains of the Christians. I want only human beings in the world. I do not want Christians in the world, Hindus in the world, Mohammedans in the world, because it makes no difference whatsoever. You only change your chains but your status of prisoner remains exactly the same. You come out of one prison and enter another. You just don't like the open sky, and I want to bring you to the open sky. So there are difficulties.

No petition came from the intelligentsia of this country. And the amazing thing is that my own people, my sannyasins... But after all their courage is also part of the shattered courage of India. I have been here for the past three days and a certain one of my well-known Indian sannyasins is not to be seen anywhere, because there is a strict order from his wife that if he comes here, her doors are closed to him. I can be dropped, but to listen to the wife is a husband's holy duty! The poor man must be writhing. This man's aunt must be here, and she should give him the message: "I never expected that you would prove yourself to be so spineless."

And those who are famous in the name of religion...I am against them all because the very things they are famous for are also so stupid that I cannot support them. A Jaina *muni* does not take a bath: I cannot support this. This is sheer stupidity. And particularly in Mumbai, which has become the main base of the Jaina *munis* and where they are drenched in perspiration, and yet they cannot take a bath because that is decoration of the body. If you want to talk to the Jaina *munis* you will have to sit far away from them because they have such a foul breath. Their bodies stink. They are such a storehouse of stink that talking to them directly and closely... We do not even

23

have this much intelligence that we can think about and reconsider anything afresh.

I have heard:

One night a man and a woman are busy making love on the bed. Suddenly the woman said, "Quick! Get up! Get up! I can hear my husband's car horn. That is my husband's horn. Quickly, hide in the closet!"

The man got up and hid himself in the closet. The car was her husband's. He came in. As the man stood inside the closet he heard a small voice. He noticed a little boy was also hiding in the same closet. The boy said, "It's very dark in here."

The man said, "Dear boy, please keep quiet. No matter how dark it may be, I am also here. Take these five rupees and keep quiet!"

The boy said, "But the darkness is too much."

The man said, "Take ten rupees, but just keep quiet!"

The boy said, "That won't do. The darkness is so great...and I am feeling so nervous that I feel like screaming."

The man had fifty rupees in his pocket, he gave them all to the boy and said, "This is the last; this is all I have – now scream or do whatsoever else you like. I don't have anything more."

The boy said, "No worries. Just keep standing still. My father doesn't stay long. He is on night shift at his job, he is about to leave. And this is my job."

The next day the boy said to his grandmother, "I want to buy a bicycle."

The grandmother replied, "A bike won't cost less than fifty rupees..."

The boy actually wanted a tricycle. He said, "Don't worry about that. I have arranged the money."

The grandmother said, "Where did you get that much money?" but the boy was not ready to disclose the source of his money.

The grandmother said, "Until you tell me that..."

She was a very religious woman – a regular Sunday churchgoer, and it was Sunday – so she said, "Come to church with me and confess to the priest where you got that money. If you don't want to tell me, that is fine, but confess it to the priest and then I will take you to the bicycle shop."

At the church the boy entered the confessional booth. As the priest appeared at the other side of the window the boy said, "Good morning. It is very dark in here."

The priest said, "You rascal! Are you starting that game again? And I don't have a penny in my pocket!"

These priests: on the one hand they will go on preaching celibacy and on the other they will continue living the opposite in their own lives. Your so-called sannyasins will go on preaching to you that to taste food is sin, that non-taste is religious, but you don't have the huge bellies that your sannyasins have. Have you seen the belly of Nityananda? If you see a photograph of Nityananda lying down you will wonder whether it is Mount Everest or a human belly. When I saw it for the first time, I was amazed! I wondered if the belly belonged to Nityananda or Nityananda belonged to the belly. And he preaches, "Non-taste is a religious act." The blind go on paying attention to these teachings, seeing his belly full well.

I am in difficulty. I want to say things exactly as I see them. That may hurt someone, but I have no intention to hurt. My intention is that some understanding arises in man – some thinking, some rationality.

I will go on moving to every nook and corner of the world.

The Catholic religion alone has got one hundred thousand missionaries; the Protestant religion has its own missionaries; Jainas have their own sannyasins; Buddhists have millions of sannyasins. I am alone, and yet it is amazing that if you have decided to be with the truth then the greatest power in the world is with you. You are not alone then; the very fundamental principle of the universe is with you. Existence is with you.

So neither am I worried about the intelligentsia nor about the religious teachers. If I have any worry it is only that I may never sell my soul, even by mistake; that I may never sell truth either, even by mistake; that I may embrace death but not part company with truth.

And I would like you all to bless me that death may become a choice but truth cannot be abandoned. I alone am enough; your blessing is enough.

Osho,
A few days before his death the famous thinker Aldous Huxley said that it is very difficult to say which of the two – the cave man or the man who is living in the skyscrapers – is more barbarous. You recently said that man has not grown much since the monkey. Please comment on this.

Take a look at man's deeds. Man has fought five thousand wars in three thousand years. His whole story is a story of killing, of burning people alive – and not just one person, thousands. And this story has not come to an end.

I was recently in Greece, for just four weeks, and the Greek Orthodox Church and its main head, the Archbishop of the Greek Orthodox Church, started spitting poison. Telegram after telegram was sent to the president, to the prime minister, to the newspapers: "If this dangerous man is not thrown out of Greece, I will burn him alive along with the house he is living in."

I had not even been out of the house. Not one of those who had come to see me was Greek. They were sannyasins from different countries of Europe who had come to see me there, and they were meeting me inside the house. What danger was there from me? And a threat to burn me alive? Do you think that man has evolved beyond the monkey? So far, no monkey has ever burnt any other monkey alive; no monkey is a Hindu or a Mohammedan or a Christian. A monkey is only a monkey.

And if this is evolution, there is no sense in such an evolution. The truth is that man has not evolved at all. He has only fallen from the trees, so you can't even match a monkey anymore: you don't even have enough power to jump from one tree to another – neither do you have the stamina, nor the youth nor the energy. And the entire story of your deeds proves that you have not become a man, you have become a demon. Yes, a demon, but hiding behind the guise of beautiful names. In the guise of being a Hindu, you can stab a Mohammedan straight in the chest – with no trouble at all. In the guise of being a Mohammedan, you can burn the temple of a Hindu who has done no harm to you – without a single worry.

In the Second World War Hitler alone killed sixty million people – and he was just one man. Would you call this evolution? The Second World War is about to finish, Germany has already surrendered, and the American President orders atomic bombing over Japan in Hiroshima and Nagasaki. Even American generals said that this was completely unnecessary, because after Germany's defeat it would have been only a matter of two weeks at the most until Japan's defeat. Even if the five year-old war had continued for another two weeks, nothing could have gone wrong. But dropping atom bombs on two big cities like Hiroshima and Nagasaki whose residents had nothing to do with the war? Two hundred thousand people turning into ash within ten minutes? And the American President who ordered this…and we haven't even changed his name yet. The name of the President was Truman – true man! At least now we should start calling him "Untruman."

And the next morning when the journalists from the newspapers asked the president, "Could you sleep alright last night?" Truman answered, "I have never slept as well as I did last night, after I had heard the news that the atom bombs had been successful."

The success of the atom bomb is important; the murder of two hundred thousand defenseless, innocent people did not worry him. Can you call him a human being?

No, there has been no evolution of man. There is only one evolution for man: that he can recognize his inner self. Without that there can be no evolution of man whatsoever. And the day I recognize my inner self, I have also recognized your inner self. The day I have known myself, I have also known all that is worth knowing in this world. And the fragrance that will be present in my life after that is the only evolution there is; the light that will be there, is the only evolution. What we have been calling evolution up until now, is no evolution. We have more material things than the monkeys have, but we don't have more soul than the monkeys.

Evolution of the inner self is the only evolution.

It is possible too that someone may be blind, but know himself. Then he is better than any man with eyes. After all, what will your eyes see? Although the man may be blind, he has seen himself, and in that moment of seeing himself, he has seen that center which is the center of the whole existence. This experience is the experience of deathlessness, is the experience of the eternal.

Only a handful of people in the history of mankind have really become man – only those few people who have experienced their selves. All the rest are men only in name. The label upon them is "man," the packaging is "man," but inside there is nothing. And if anything is there, it is poison – full of jealousy, full of hatred, full of destruction, full of violence.

In the final analysis I only want to say this to you: that if there is even an iota of intelligence in your life then accept the challenge. Do not allow yourself to be taken to the graveyard without having realized your self. Yes, once you know yourself, even if your death happens today rather than tomorrow, it will not matter, because for the one who has known himself, no death exists.

The experience of deathlessness is the only evolution.

Thank you.

CHAPTER 3

THE SEEDS TO THE
FLOWERS:
CREATING THE MILIEU

Just minutes ago I was looking at your questions.

It saddens me to know that India's intelligence has fallen into such a muddy mire that it can't even ask questions. And the kind of questions it asks are rotten; they stink.

If you want, I will answer. But then brace your hearts. If you are hit, don't be disturbed. And not a word should be edited out from what I say, not a word should be added to what I say, so that your reality is revealed not only in front of India but in front of the whole world. If even asking questions is so difficult, there is not much hope that you will understand the answers.

But I will try. Now start.

Osho,
Which is the best country in the world?
And which do you believe to be the worst country?

India is both – because I am here, and you are also here. India has touched the heights of consciousness, and now I also see you in the gutters. And you have become so accustomed to the gutters that you have turned them into temples. You don't even want to get out of them.

When the revolution happened in France, there was a central prison there, the Bastille, where only prisoners sentenced for a life term were kept. Their handcuffs and fetters were only broken after they had died. Once their handcuffs and fetters were locked onto them, the keys were thrown down a well. Thousands of heavily chained prisoners had been living in the dark cells of the Bastille.

When the revolution happened the idea naturally came in the revolutionaries' minds to free these prisoners; that this should be their first act because these prisoners had suffered the most. They broke down the gates of the Bastille, but the prisoners of the Bastille were not ready to leave the prison – because someone had been there for sixty years, someone for fifty years, with no responsibility, with food at fixed times, even if it was rubbish. And after such a long time those fetters had become part of their bodies.

But revolutionaries are stubborn people. They forcibly cut off their handcuffs and the fetters, and set the people of the Bastille free. Those prisoners came out of the prison crying and saying, "Where are we to go? By now we have forgotten any names and addresses; by now we have forgotten even those people who once knew us. Perhaps they may not even be alive anymore – our wives, our children. What has happened to them? Where did they go? We have no idea at all. There will be no shelter to sleep under, no food to eat, no bedding to use – a forced revolution!"

One thing is very difficult in this world; a forced revolution is a very difficult thing. Revolution is a flower. Either it flowers within you or it doesn't, but no one can force it to flower.

By the evening almost half of the prisoners had come back to the prison. They said, "We remained hungry the whole day. Nobody was ready to give us a job, we are no longer capable of working, and neither did we receive any human respect. And the biggest problem is that those chains that were put on our hands forever, those fetters that were put on our legs forever – thirty years ago, forty years ago, fifty years ago – now we cannot fall asleep without them. Their weight has become associated with our sleep. Forgive us, and allow us to go back to our dark cells. We don't like this light outside."

You are asking, "Which country is the best and which is the worst?"

Countries don't exist. "Country" is a lie, "nation" is man's invention. The reality is man. This country has touched the highest peaks in Gautam Buddha, in the seers of the Upanishads, in Mahavira, in Adinatha. That, too, is India. Actually the whole of India should be that. And then there is another India: of the politicians, of the thieves; of the black-marketeers. There is an India within India.

So the question is not which country is the best and which country is the worst. The question is in which country the maximum number of good people live and in which country the maximum number of bad people live. In India both are present.

So with one hand I want very much to raise the flag of India's glory, but with the other I also want to crush it.

I do not consider India a singular unit. Hence, for me the question is meaningless. It depends on you.

I have been around the whole world. Good people are everywhere and bad people are everywhere, but everywhere the bad people are in power and the good people are powerless. Goodness has a weakness: goodness is not aggressive, goodness is not violent. Badness is aggressive, violent. Badness dominates and goodness doesn't get a chance.

The second specialty of goodness is it has no desire for recognition. Goodness is in itself such a pleasant experience that nothing more is needed, nor anything can be added to it. Badness is ambitious. So, if you want to see the bad people – politics is the place to look. And if you want to see the good people – then look for the peaceful, silent and meditating people.

The world is divided into two types, not two types of countries. The bad people are dominating and the good people are so good that they don't even ask them not to. Actually, even being dominated doesn't make a difference to the good, because the shower of their bliss, their love, their nectar is happening *within* them.

Your question is wrong; and a wrong question cannot have a right answer.

Osho,
You just said that the world is divided into two types: the good
and the bad. You went out of India in search of goodness.
How much goodness and how much badness did you get to
see during your recent travels?

Which idiot has told you that I went out of India in search of goodness?
Or is it your own invention?

...If goodness and badness are both here in India...

First answer my question. This is not an ordinary press conference
on politics. You will leave from here thoroughly shattered.
    Who told you that I had gone out of India in search of goodness?
I had gone out to spread goodness. And I found good people and I
also found bad people. And my conclusion is that it makes no difference where you live. What makes the difference is who you are.No
one is good or bad because of *zameen*, the land, but because of
zameer, the heart.

Osho,
From what you have experienced in the past thirty-two years,
after living both in India and abroad, is there any significant
change in your thoughts about India, America, religion, sex,
and the problems of India and their solutions?

Great change has come, because I am not a rotting stagnant pond.
I am a flowing Ganges. I am moving forward each moment.
    The famous thinker of Greece, Heraclites, has said, "You cannot
step in the same river twice." Some day, in some world, in eternity,
I am going to meet Heraclites, and then I want to say to him that
you cannot step in the same river even once, because the river is

33

continuously flowing. By the time you touch the upper surface of the river, the lower surface has flowed away. And by the time you arrive at the lower surface, the upper surface has flowed away.

The seed is the same – it has become the tree, the foliage and the blossoming flowers. In my life I haven't grown in opposition to anything. Rather whatever I have said, I have only refined it more and more. So I will certainly not say the same things that I was saying thirty years ago.

Thirty years ago I was talking of the seeds; now I am showering the flowers.

Osho,
Seeing that instead of becoming liberated man's soul has become
full of fear because of taboos born out of so-called religions
and spiritual traditions, what plans do you have in your
program for human liberation?

Human liberation is like man's health. The diseases can be different – someone is suffering from TB, someone from a cold, someone from a fever or cancer – the diseases can be thousands, but health itself is just one. There are not many kinds of health. Human liberation is man's ultimate health, his ultimate flowering. It is the fragrance arising out of his life.

As a result of thousands of years of continuously searching, man has discovered the science of this too. I call this science meditation. No man can ever experience liberation except through meditation. Neither can prayer take you toward liberation, because in prayer from the very beginning you are accepting a basic lie: you are believing that God exists. You don't know him, you have no acquaintance with him – if you were to meet God on the way you wouldn't be able to recognize him. And because prayer is extrovert, it is worldly.

There is one more journey – that of meditation – which is introvert, in which you set out in search of yourself, in which you make getting acquainted with yourself your journey. And the day one becomes acquainted with oneself, authentic benediction showers in your life. And that showering rain is one and the same. That rain does not bother to see if this is the roof of a Mohammedan, of a Hindu or of a Jaina. What has a rain cloud to do with that? Just your readiness is required.

And the key to meditation is very small. All keys are small. The small key to meditation is that there is so much peace within that not a ripple of thought stirs; such a silence within that no wave arises; such an emptiness that only you are and there is nothing else; where there is not even a feeling of "I am." In that very moment this whole existence becomes godliness and it showers upon you.

Godliness is not something that requires a search. Those who set out in search of godliness are under an illusion. What capacity have you to search for godliness? You have no previous acquaintance, you don't know its name, you don't know its form or color. Godliness searches for you.

There is an ancient Egyptian proverb that when a disciple is ready, the master appears. With a slight change, it can be put this way: whenever you become peaceful, empty and silent, your inner being is filled with the bliss and the beauty of godliness. Except for this, there has never been ever any other way, nor will there ever be.

Osho,
You have said that you have never lied in your whole life, but for the sake of your people you had to lie to get yourself released. Osho, the saints have had to pass through a phase of fire tests – were you not supposed to do the same?

I have lied three times in my life. Who told you that I have never lied?

You said so in an interview that you gave to Dharmayuga.

There must be some mistake on the part of *Dharmayuga*. I have lied three times.

When?

Because to me, love and compassion are the most precious things, once I lied to protect Anand Sheela. I had explained to her a thousand times that no adoption of me had ever occurred, but she prepared false documents so that a case could be made for my staying in America. The question before me was of an old man, of Sheela, and of a commune of thousands of sannyasins. I lied only this much: I said that I had no idea and that I may have been adopted in my childhood, but it had never been told to me.

The second time I lied was in the American jails, after having been harassed for twelve days in every way. The American government told my attorneys that there were only two options: "One option is that this case runs on in the courts for years. We know that we will lose the case, because Osho has not done anything wrong. But, the case may run for ten years, fifteen years, twenty years. During this time we will destroy the commune. Without Osho the commune will die, and the movement of sannyasins will be destroyed all over the world." The second option: If I accepted – they had prepared a list of one hundred and thirty-six crimes against me, all false – if I pleaded guilty on any two counts, the movement could survive, the commune could survive; all the sannyasins spread all over the world could continue.

This was blackmail. My attorneys had tears in their eyes. They said, "We know that this is all false, but by accepting two crimes this whole turmoil can come to an end. So two crimes… I only spoke two words in the American court – both lies. And I spoke them telling the judge that I was lying on the oath of truth. I said that I had produced false documents in order to get entry into America, and that I had arranged sham marriages of my sannyasins so that they could stay in America. Neither had I arranged anybody's marriage nor did I produce any false documents.

Except on these three occasions I have never told a lie. And for these three lies I am not ashamed. I am proud, because these lies were told for some great vision. And these lies were not for some personal gain of mine. Except for these three lies, my whole life has been only for truth – no matter how costly it may have proved to me; no matter that I may have risked my life. I have always been ready for those things.

There have been many attempts on my life – in India, in America. And now America wants…it is ready to give five million rupees to any-one who kills me. I have sent a message to Ronald Reagan that why implicate some poor guy, because if he kills me he might get caught and have to face the law. Just give that five million rupees to our work, to meditation, and I am ready to die – a straightforward deal!

As I see it, the decisive factor between truth and lies is not the truth or the lie itself. The decisive factor is the intention. All three times I have told the lies for the sake of others, not for myself. For myself, I am ready to die. There is no question of telling a lie.

Osho,
You said that the three times you told lies were for others.
The movement that you have led over the past thirty-two years,
the community that you have been guiding, the thinking and
the philosophy that you have been propagating… Up until now,
hasn't any person in the whole community advanced to such
a point that you start to think of what will happen to the
commune after you, to your whole philosophy and thought?
Will you give this some thought, whether any person is
prepared or will be prepared to spread your entire thinking and
philosophy here and abroad after you have gone?

I do not prepare people because prepared people are of no use. Coached people do not get entry into the temple of life. There are many friends who are getting ready, but I am not preparing them. I am only creating the milieu. A gardener does not create the rose flowers; he only prepares the soil, sows the seeds, puts the manure – the flowers come on their own. I have no intention of imposing myself on any person. That I call spiritual slavery. Whatsoever I can do to prepare the soil, I am doing. In it, those who have even a bit of soul, their flowers will bloom – in this life, in the next life, in some other life.

But if in the process of preparing this soil, I had to tell lies three times, I am not ashamed. It is the government of America that should be ashamed: this is not justice. I was ready to fight the case in the courts. It is the first time that an individual was standing against the biggest power of the world. They, not me, had called the case the United States of America versus Bhagwan Shree Rajneesh! I had already won it. And still they had to lie and had to present the lie in such a tricky way that my attorneys said – with tears in their eyes, touching my feet – "We have never seen anything like this in our lives. The two options that they are giving us are both full of malice. The case can be prolonged, your work can be stopped."

Even if I fall into hell because I have told a lie, I have no objection. But I would like the soil that I am preparing to be ready, for some flowers to bloom, for some streams to come alive, for some stars to rise.

This was the first time – with my case – that the American government invited the attorneys for a negotiation, otherwise it is always the attorneys who request the government for some negotiations. The American government was willing for there to be a settlement and there were reasons why.

Two days ago that truth accidentally came out of the American attorney general's mouth. He was asked in a press conference: "Why was Osho not sentenced?" He gave three reasons: "One, we wanted to destroy Osho's movement, his commune; that was our first priority. Second, we have no evidence against Osho that he has committed any crime."

This is a very interesting world. I have not committed any crime but I have been fined six million rupees – just to show to the world that I must have committed some crime. Otherwise, why should I be fined?

And the third point is even more significant. The American attorney general who is the highest authority of the legal system there said, "We did not want Osho to become a martyr, because that mistake has been made before."

Socrates could not be killed by poisoning. Two thousand five hundred years have passed; Socrates is more alive than ever. The murderers have gone into oblivion, even their names are forgotten. When Jesus was crucified he had only ten or twelve disciples; after the crucifixion the figure went on growing. Al-Hillaj Mansoor was cut into pieces, but that does not cut the soul. There have been other Sufis of the same caliber, but Al-Hillaj Mansoor shines like a polar star. "We did not want to make Osho a martyr, a polar star. Anyway our purpose is fulfilled."

Still they made a last attempt, because as I came out of the jail – the court had freed me because there was no crime against me and no law was against me – it was necessary for me to go back to the jail to pick up my things, my clothes and complete the formalities. I was surprised to see that there was complete silence in the jail. There was not a single person on the ground floor office of the jail. I even said, "I have passed through here so many times. There is always such a bustle here: high-level officials, jailers – what has happened today? Is there a holiday to celebrate my release?"

The person who was taking me had sweat on his forehead – in an air-conditioned jail! I said, "Wipe off your sweat, because sweat also says much."

He took me to the place in the office where I was to receive my belongings. There was not a single person there. Before, I had never seen fewer than a dozen people always there. And that man said to me, "I'll have to get my officer's signature, so I am going out briefly. Make yourself comfortable here."

Five minutes, ten minutes, fifteen minutes passed – and no trace of that man. And he had locked the door from the outside. I was alone in the room.

When I came out of the jail I found out that there had been a time bomb under the chair I was sitting on. But they couldn't set the time bomb accurately because they did not know how long the case was going to take in the court. And to the judge it was clear that there was nothing in the case, so it was all over in five minutes. They might have guessed that I would return by five o'clock in the evening, but I returned too soon.

Now no one else except for the government can put a time bomb in that inner room of the jail; no outsider can reach there.

What was the fear? What was the fear behind their effort to kill me? And what my attorneys said was that if I did not accept any two small crimes, they did not expect that I would come out of the jail alive. The case would be intentionally prolonged; opportunities would be sought inside the jail...and opportunities *were* sought inside the jails.

In one jail I was kept with a person who was dying and had a terribly infectious disease that had no cure. No one had been kept in his cell for the past six months. That man wrote me a note on a small piece of paper: "Before you touch anything here, call the doctor and the jailer and ask why you have been put here. I am dying and it is an indirect device to kill you too – so that you do not become a martyr, a messiah, and you die from a disease instead."

Just imagine: if Jesus had died on his bed, as ninety-nine percent of people die, there would have been no Christianity in the world.

It took me an hour of knocking on the cell door before the doctor came. I asked the doctor, "When nobody has been put in this cell for the past six months because you have been against that happening, why was I put in this cell today when you were present, in front of your eyes? And why did you not object? Are you a doctor or a murderer?

In another jail I was asked not to write my name on the form as I entered jail, but to write "David Washington" instead.

I said, "David Washington is not my name. I can remain sitting here in this office the whole night, but David Washington is not my name and I will not write it. And you will also have to stay awake the whole night with me in this office. It was midnight, the man himself was one of the US Marshals, and on his coat was the inscription: "Department of Justice."

I said to him "At least, take that coat off! Fill in the form and I will sign it."

He thought it was a good compromise. He filled in the form in his own writing and I wrote my signature on it in Hindi. He looked at the paper from all angles and said, "What is this?"

I said, "David Copperfield, David Washington – whatsoever you want to make out of it, you can. This is my signature. And you look after the Department of Justice and you can't even understand this much. I have at least enough intelligence to conclude why you don't want my name on the form: so that if you kill me in this jail, there will be no trace of me, of where I disappeared to. That's why the handwriting is now yours and the signature is mine. You have arranged your own hanging!"

At 5 a.m. I was transferred to another jail, because that form had to be destroyed.

I am not worried about such matters, because whatsoever life can offer I have received. Now there is no question of receiving anything more from life. But there are tens of thousands of people in the world who are being prepared. I want to live for their preparation.

I told a lie in the service of truth.

Osho,
Eight months ago, after the American episode, in an interview with India Today *you said that because Rajiv Gandhi is a non-political man, he could be expected to do some good work. In your interview the day before yesterday, you expressed some disappointment about the way Rajiv Gandhi is operating. Could you elaborate on this?*

I am not a politician, but this much I know: who is a shoemaker and who can make good shoes. Rajiv is a good pilot, but being a good pilot is no certificate for being a good prime minister. And the coming elections will decide this.

Rajiv Gandhi has exploited the murder of Indira Gandhi to the full. Rajiv Gandhi is the prime minister of India on the bloodstains of his mother. Here we want people who give blood, not people who sell even their own mother's blood. Rajiv has his own capabilities, his own talents. He should use them.

41

And while Indira Gandhi was alive I sent a message to Rajiv saying, "If you ever wish to get into politics, start training now, start by sitting at the feet of your mother." The answer I received was: "I am the sole earning member of the whole family..." Sanjay was already dead "...and if Indira loses her power, there is no one else except me to provide even food for the family. Moreover, I have no interest in politics." Did you ever hear that Rajiv might have taken any interest in politics while Indira Gandhi was alive? That he might have learnt even the *abc* of politics? A coterie of boys is riding on the chest of the country, and they will be blown to pieces by the coming elections. Lies and trickery need long practice.

The leader of the opposition party asked in parliament: "Why did Osho have to leave India again when he had just returned? Had conditions been imposed on him so that he could not leave India, so that his sannyasins from outside India could not come here to visit him, and especially so that the news media and the journalists from outside India wouldn't be allowed to reach him?" And with this I thought, "What then will be the difference between that American jail and this Indian jail?"

At least in the first American jail the sheriff had been reading my books, had been listening to my talks. He was so interested that, putting all laws and rules aside, he called a world press conference inside the jail for me. In America I could talk inside the jail to journalists of the world press against the American government. And in India – even remaining free – I will not be able to meet journalists, and those who love me will not be able to come to me. So there is no sense in my remaining or not remaining here.

The leader of the opposition party in India asked if these were the conditions that were put on Osho: that his disciples would not be able to come to see him. And the government of Rajiv Gandhi said, "This is untrue. His disciples can come to see him." Then I asked many of my sannyasins in different countries to go to the embassies for a visa. Everywhere they were refused.

This is amazing! Here, the government says that they can come, and to the embassies they give the instruction that none of my people should be allowed to come to India. These lies and deceptions cannot elevate this country.

And the people who are in power today are so impotent that they cannot even say to the country, for its own good, such a thing as "Reduce your population; adopt birth control." They are pushing the country toward death.

You will be surprised to know that India is starving and its wheat is being sold outside India, because with that money, nuclear power and its accoutrements can be bought. No one is interested in your stomach. This country will die of poverty and Rajiv Gandhi will be responsible for it. Today you may kill people in Punjab to suppress them, but in how many places can you kill?

Rajiv has no personality, no message or charisma to keep this country together. Assam wants to separate. Tomorrow Tamil Nadu will want to separate. There are thirty languages in this country – they will all want to separate into thirty different countries.

Let me remind you that for thousands of years India has not been one nation. In the times of Gautam Buddha, twenty-five centuries ago, there were five thousand kingdoms in this country. It has been the Mohammedans, the Moghuls, the Turks, the Hoonas and the English who have forcibly kept you united. But now you cannot be kept forcibly united. Now, you can only be kept united through love. Now, only one bond can keep this nation together and that is of love – neither of language nor of religion nor of province, rather only of love.

What message of love does Rajiv have? What message of meditation does Rajiv have? The parliament of India is retarded. Any one of these guys can be tested for their IQ and it will be very difficult for a single one of them to cross the mental age of fourteen. This country has been left in the hands of senseless boys. This situation will have to be changed.

There are sensible people in this country, there are also intelligent people in this country – people who have no political ambitions, and yet have compassion in their hearts for this country. But there is a difficulty. Those who are ambitious inevitably suffer from an inferiority complex. In order to hide their inferiority, they try to reach to high positions. And those who are not suffering from an inferiority complex – who are content, delighted in themselves – do not go begging for votes. Drop your hopes that this country can be helped to rise by beggars. We will have to change course. We will have to go to those contented people who could put this country back on track and appeal to them. They will not come to you asking for votes.

And there is no shortage of these people.

So, I have changed in my point of view completely.

I was in American jails for twelve days. Rajiv did not do a single thing through the Indian ambassador, he did not even ask what my crime was, and why I had been arrested without reason and without an arrest warrant, and why I was being dragged from jail to jail without being taken to a court.

No, nobody wants to annoy America. They are all beggars. They want all the necessary supplies from America so that they can create nitrogen bombs, so that they can create death rays. Nobody is interested in life.

It was the duty of Rajiv Gandhi to raise his voice if an Indian was being forcibly persecuted without any crime, without any reason. There were voices from other countries of the world, but India remained silent. And the day I came out of jail, a man from the Indian embassy came and asked: "Of what service can we be to you?"

I said, "Where were you for twelve days? Do you use opium? Do you smoke hashish? Where were you for these twelve days? Where was your government, where was your ambassador?"

The answer that that man gave was: "We were observing the situation to see what was happening?"

I said, "By the time your observation had been completed, I would have been dead. Were you going to come to ask my dead body, 'Of what service can we be to you?' Go and tell your ambassador, tell your prime minister, that I do not need their services. Yes, if they ever need my services, I am available."

I am compelled to call this government a childish, unadult, immature government. Such a vast country, where the population is around one billion, is not free enough of danger to be left in the hands of these children. This is not dealing with Diwali fire-crackers: it is a question of the life and death of a whole nation.

I want this country to be put in the hands of intelligent people. I want there to be no political parties in this country. There is no need for any political party: what is needed are intelligent people whom we elect and who can take collective decisions for the future of this country.

I am an anarchist. Political parties only exploit. For five years one party exploits, and by that time people have forgotten about the exploitations of the other party. Then, that party comes into power and for five years that party exploits – by which time people have forgotten about the exploitations of the first party. This is a very interesting game. The boys are playing and there is no referee.

Osho,
The role of physical contact has played a significant part in your techniques for the spiritual search. At least, that is the way you used to conduct things in India – I have no idea how it was in America. If these same methods are to continue, then in view of the new danger of AIDS, are you thinking of bringing any change to these techniques?

AIDS is a religious disease. It was born in the monasteries and at those places where religious leaders were teaching celibacy to people.

Celibacy is absolutely unnatural. The only way to be a celibate is to have surgery. Only an impotent person can be celibate, nobody else can. And even today the teaching of celibacy continues. People like Mahatma Gandhi teach: "Celibacy is life," and toward the end of his life, at the age of seventy, he came to realize that no, celibacy is not life, and started sleeping with a naked woman.

Physical relationship is natural. If it is kept natural, there is no danger of AIDS. So far, no AIDS has been discovered in forest animals. But in the zoos, AIDS is rampant, because if only male monkeys are there. If there is no female, then even monkeys have as much intelligence as your monks and sannyasins have – some way will have to be found. You eat food, and if someone were to say to you that urinating is prohibited, you will be in difficulty. You will drink water – what will you do with the urine? In secret you will find some way and will deceive yourself and deceive the whole society.

If AIDS spreads in India, it will be through your religious leaders. In the West it is also spreading through them and it is spreading rapidly.

You can separate man and woman, but what will you do with the sperm energy that is being created in you? Your sac of the sperm has a certain limit, after that...after that it will take any unnatural, perverted form, or you will have wet dreams.

Even at the age of seventy, Mahatma Gandhi used to have wet dreams, but we are so blind that we can't even imagine this. Mahatma Gandhi was an honest man. I have no doubts about his honesty. But if one is having wet dreams at the age of seventy, this only means one thing – that it is beyond your control. Hunger comes; it is not in your hands.

All that is essential in nature has not been left in your hands, otherwise you would have died long ago. You breathe, but it is not in your hands, otherwise in the night you might forget to breathe. In the big crowds on the roads you would forget to breathe.

The sexual energy that is created within you, within all men and women, is created from your blood. If you don't want it to be created, then blood has not to be created. You will have to go to the very roots. And for blood not to be created, you will have to stop eating. So if you are determined to be a celibate then go and hang yourself from a tree; and hang a placard around your neck: "I am a celibate"!

The only way for AIDS to be prevented is for the enmity, the antagonism that we have created between man and woman over thousands of years to be dropped. If we can drop it, then there will be no question of AIDS. AIDS is not born out of heterosexual intercourse. AIDS is born out of homosexual intercourse, and such a man, if he makes love to a woman, will give AIDS to that woman also. And the disease of AIDS is the ultimate disease.

So far, no disease like it has been known. There is no cure for it. Scientists say that for at least ten years we cannot even expect a cure to be found. And it is spreading so rapidly, and neither can you tell someone that you have AIDS nor can you go to a doctor – nor does the doctor want you to come to him: "Be kind to me; you can take a fee from me, but go back home!" Nor is any hospital happy to admit AIDS patients, because AIDS spreads not only through physical sexual contact, but through sweat, through saliva, through tears.

There is only one race in the world, the Eskimos, who from the very beginning have never kissed. When the Christian missionaries arrived for the first time to convert the Eskimos, the Eskimos had to laugh so much. They could not imagine what kind of dirty thing these missionaries were doing. It is a dirty act; putting your tongue in each other's mouths, mixing the other's saliva in your mouth. And you do all this so tastily! But the AIDS virus can be in the saliva. Every substance that comes out of the body can carry the AIDS virus.

There is only one way: to declare celibacy illegal. Catch hold of every single monk and get them all married. Otherwise it is possible that even before a nuclear war happens, AIDS may finish humanity. If the AIDS patient is kept in complete safety, still he cannot live more than a few years. This is the longest period. And how will you keep him in complete safety? After all he will have to do some work, he will have to meet people.

The ability of an AIDS patient's immune system to fight against any disease becomes zero. If he catches cold, even the cold doesn't get better. If he has a fever, the fever doesn't get cured. No medicine works on such a person. Medicine has a way of working: when we give someone some medicine, his body supports the medicine. With their combined efforts the disease is removed. The body of an AIDS patient does not provide any support at all. It is hollow. You go on pouring medicine into it, but it is meaningless. If you had poured that medicine into a gutter it would have had the same effect on him as it had when you injected it into his body.

But the religions of the world still go on preaching that without celibacy no one can ever reach to the ultimate truth; that celibacy is essential. These are the enemies of the country and the enemies of society. It is necessary to stop them and bring men and women closer so that men and men do not start indulging in sex, so that women and women do not start indulging in sex.

When I was in America, the Texan government passed a law in their legislative assembly saying that homosexual sex is illegal, and that ten years' imprisonment is the minimum punishment. You won't believe it: a procession of one million people protested saying, "This is an attack on our freedom."

Instead of declaring celibacy illegal, they declared homosexuality illegal. Its outcome will be very dangerous. What it means is that homosexuality will go underground and you will not know about it. You will not even know if wiping away the tears from a small child who was crying was an act of compassion or of murder – because it is possible that the contact of your hands with his tears is giving birth to yet another case of AIDS.

And the latest news is that many newly born babies are born with AIDS. Three children were found AIDS positive at the time of their birth.

This is the deadliest disease that man has ever seen in the whole history of mankind.

My thoughts have matured even more about man living a spontaneous, easy, and natural life. Otherwise perversion will be the simple outcome.

I have heard that a grand female elephant was passing through the forest and a *munda*, a monk, came running after her. The elephant asked, "Oh Munde, why are you following me?"

The monk said, "Mother – you are so big that I have to call you what else but 'mother' – there is only one desire left in my life and it is because of it that I am still wandering in the world. If you can help me a little, I can soon be living in *moksha*, the realm of liberation."

The elephant said, "I am willing to help. What is it that you want?"

The monk said, "I am ashamed of saying this, but nobody is around here and no one will ever come to know of it. I don't know why this idea comes to my mind again and again, but what would it be like to make love to a female elephant?"

The elephant said, "Love? You will make love to me? Alright, have you brought the ladder, etcetera?"

The monk said, "Yes, I have brought the municipality's ladder. That is what I am running with, huffing and puffing. If you could fulfill this small desire of mine, I can be freed from this cycle of lives upon lives. This will not leave my mind: I have seen everything, but I have never made love to a female elephant."

Now I understand why male and female elephants are kept in the monasteries.

She said, "Hurry up! Be finished! I also have a date. My boyfriend must be waiting for me. Oh Munde, climb your ladder."

The *munda* got busy lovemaking.

And what lovemaking – it was a kind of physical exercise! Making push-ups, and he was drenched in sweat. And then a coconut fell from the tree right above the head of the elephant. She said, "Ahh!!!"

The *munda* said, "Excuse me, my beloved. Am I hurting you?"

The female elephant said, "I can't feel you at all. Have you started yet or not?"

The *munda* said, "I finished long ago. This is my guru named 'Gunda,' the hooligan, who is sitting at the top of the tree. In my cult the guru is called 'gunda.' Although he is in absolute support of celibacy, seeing this amazing scene that could not even be seen in Hindi movies, he got so excited, forgot all about celibacy and when nothing else came to his mind he started shaking the tree vigorously. This coconut has fallen on your head because of his grace."

This society of *gundas* and *mundas* has given you a thousand and one types of diseases. What I envision is a spontaneous, natural, non-artificial life. The more natural you are, the more peace there will be in your life; the more the possibility of attaining to that nectar which we have been waiting for centuries for, for life after life.

So except me – and I repeat, except me – neither your pope nor the Ayatollah Khomeni nor your shankaracharyas, nor your Acharya Tulsi – no one can save you from AIDS. There is only one way to be protected from AIDS. Become simple, straightforward; do not unnecessarily try to stand on your head. Nature has given you feet, simply walk with them.

In India AIDS is spreading amongst the soldiers, in the colleges where the girls and the boys are being forced to live in separate hostels, and in the monasteries where a wall is created between the men and women. It is very strange that you oppose what nature has given you. And then you are afraid to suffer the consequences of the opposition. And hundreds of thousands of people are falling victim to the disease of AIDS everyday. That is a gift of Christianity. India can still be saved and the path can still be changed.

But my difficulty is that when I say things exactly as they are in their nakedness, I have made arrangements for my own stoning. You do not want to hear truth. You want to go on chanting "Rama, Rama, Rama," and for celibacy to happen. It did not happen to Ramachandra himself, how can it happen to you? Just think, the person you worship, Krishna, held sixteen thousand women captive in his house.

Yes, it is immoral behavior, but at least it did not cause AIDS.

Osho,
My last question is – and I expect a specific answer to it – what is your program now that you have come back to India? Where will you live and what will be your style of functioning?

You should ask this question to my friend in whose house I am a guest. I am a rather stubborn kind of a man, so if I decide not to leave this house, I simply won't. My friend can find a new house for himself!

CHAPTER 4

AN

EXPERIENCE

OF DEATHLESSNESS

Osho,
I am at a loss in how to understand myself?
And I have a tremendous fear of death.

Who doesn't have a fear of death? Everyone thinks that it is always somebody else who is dying. And there is a point in this logic because we never see ourselves dying, it is always others that we see dying. We take others' bodies to the crematorium, and later have a bath in the river and happily come back home, wondering: "Could it be that I am an exception?"

The cemetery is always built outside a town. It should be built exactly in the middle of the town so that everyone can clearly see that someone or other is dying every day and the queue that he himself has been standing in is shortening fast – his own turn is close at hand. But we build the cemetery outside the town: a person has died, now forget it, let it go! When someone dies and a funeral procession is passing by, we pull our children inside the house so that they don't come to know about death. But this kind of deception won't do. He who is born will have to die. Whatever has one pole is bound to have the other pole as well.

If you feel afraid of death, then try to know life. There is no other way. Fear of death is proof of the fact that so far you haven't experienced life. I have heard that many people only come to realize this upon their death: "My God! I have been alive all this time!" Life simply passes away in worthless activities.

Devote at least an hour every day to yourself – to the search for your life. For at least an hour sit down in peace, in silence. Forget that you are a Hindu, a Mohammedan, a Jaina, a Christian. Forget that you are a woman, a man; forget that you are a child, an old man – just forget the whole world.

Slowly an experience of the eternal starts arising from within you. The Hindu in you dies – he will have to. The man in you dies, the woman in you dies, the child in you dies, the young man in you dies, the Mohammedan in you dies.... Separate yourself for an hour every day from all those things that die, and try to search within yourself: that is there anything else other than these things? And thousands of people, without exception, have experienced that there is a spring of eternal life within you all. The day you taste even a drop of it, your fear of death will disappear.

This fear of death is a good thing. It keeps you awake. If there were no fear of death in man, there would be no possibility at all of men like Buddha and Mahavira being born in the world. This is the kindness of death toward you, that it does not let you rest. Once in a while it reminds you that one day you will have to die. Now old age starts taking over – and what else but death is there in the next stage? And before death knocks on your door, try to make some acquaintance with that which is deathless.

And to take one hour out of twenty-four for yourself every day is not a great deal. How much time do you take out for foolishnesses? I have seen people playing cards. You ask, "What are you doing?" and the answer is: "We are passing the time." Fools! Are you passing the time or yourselves? Who has ever been able to pass the time? People are running toward the movie houses: there is a crowd there, there are fights at the ticket windows. You ask, "What are you doing?" And the answer is: "To pass the time. Three hours will pass happily."

Who knows in how many other trivial things you go on "passing the time." You are passing the time in useless gossip with friends without realizing that this very time can also give you an experience of deathlessness.

And I don't ask you to renounce everything and escape to the Himalayas. Nothing will come out of that. Sitting on the Himalayas, you will still be thinking of your chess moves.

Be where you are: just take one hour. You are giving twenty-three hours to the world – what is this miserliness about giving one hour to existence? Give one hour, sitting on your bed just before going to sleep. And it won't be long before you are in contact with your interiority within, where the Ganges of life is flowing like an inner river. Before it dries up, it is necessary to make your acquaintance with it. The fear of death will disappear, because then you will know that death simply doesn't occur.

Death is the greatest fiction in this world. Only bodies are changed, homes are changed, clothes are changed – but your essence remains forever the same. But you will have to make the acquaintance of this essence. Except for making this acquaintance, there is no other meaning to religion. And this will not happen by going to the *gurudwaras* or the mosques or the temples either, because there, too, you will do the same unfortunate things. After all, it will be *you* there. Now if a beautiful woman suddenly comes into your sight, how will you be able to resist bumping your body against hers? And such a sacred act certainly is befitting to a sacred place like a temple!

No, in this very world – where all sorts of nonsense is going on – lies the real opportunity, the real test, the fire test. Right here, for an hour every day at any time…. And it is also not that this time has to be a fixed one. People seek excuses of all sorts: that it is very difficult to have a fixed time. I don't ask you to fix a time…whenever it is possible. But just remember one thing: that in twenty-four hours, one hour is yours. And the realization, the experiencing of all the realities of life – just in that one hour – will free you from the fear of death.

Know life. Then there is no death at all.

Al Hillaj Mansoor was a famous Sufi mystic who was driven to death by Mohammedans, cutting him limb by limb because he was saying things that went against the Koran – not against religion though, but books are a very small phenomenon: religion does not fit into them. Al Hillaj Mansoor had only one proclamation: "*Anal'haq,*" in other words, "I am the whole." And this was beyond the tolerance of the Mohammedans – that someone should call himself "the whole." The torturous death that they gave to Mansoor...no other man in this world has ever been put through this.

Two events happened on that day.

Junnaid, the guru of Mansoor, must have been merely a teacher – the kind of guru that can be purchased by the dozen and who is present everywhere, in each and every village. They whisper anything in your ears and they become a guru to you. So, Junnaid was telling him, "Look, your experience that you are the whole may be true, but don't say it."

Al Hillaj replied, "This is beyond my capacity, because when I am enveloped in ecstasy, and when the rainclouds of ecstatic delight overtake me, then neither you are in my remembrance nor Mohammedans nor the world; neither life nor death. It is not that then I proclaim 'Anal haq.' No, then the proclamation simply happens. This experience is running in my every life's breath."

Finally Al Hillaj was caught.

The day he was caught, he was circumambulating himself, walking around himself in circles. People asked him, "What are you doing? This is the time to go on a pilgrimage to the Kaaba and for circumambulating the sacred stone of the Kaaba. And here you are standing and circumambulating your own self!"

Mansoor said, "No stone can experience 'I am the whole,' but I do. So if I circumambulate myself, the pilgrimage to Kaaba is complete. Without going anywhere, sitting in my own house, I have invited godliness into my own courtyard."

A man speaking such truths invariably falls into trouble.

Mansoor was hanging on the gallows, stones were being thrown at him, but he kept on laughing. Junnaid, too, was standing in the crowd and he was afraid that if he did not throw something at Mansoor the crowd would presume that he was in support of Mansoor. So he had secretly brought a flower; he couldn't throw a stone because he knew that what Mansoor was saying was his inner experience – and if others are unable to understand it, that is their fault. So he hit Mansoor by throwing the flower at him.

As long as stones were hitting Mansoor, he was laughing, but the moment the flower hit him, tears started to flow from his eyes. Someone asked, "What? Stones make you laugh and flowers make you cry?"

Mansoor said, "Those who are throwing stones are ignorant people. The one who has thrown the flower carries the illusion that he knows. I feel pity for him. I have nothing with me other than my tears to give to him."

And when his legs were chopped off, his hands were chopped off, he looked up toward the sky and gave a loud belly laughter. His bloodied body, a crowd of hundreds of thousands of people... People asked, "Why are you laughing?"

Mansoor said, "I am saying to existence, 'What a game you are showing me.' So much fuss and bother to kill the one who cannot die. You are unnecessarily wasting so many people's time. And I am also laughing that he whom you are killing is not me. And that which I am, you cannot even touch. Your swords cannot cut it. Your fire cannot burn it."

Once even a brief contact is established with one's life stream, the fear of death disappears.

What is the difference between ego and taking a pride in oneself?

Taking a pride in oneself is not ego. Not only is there a difference between them, they are opposites.

Ego is the feeling of being superior to others. Ego is a disease. How many people can you believe yourself to be superior to? Someone is more beautiful, someone is healthier, someone is more talented, someone is a genius. An egoist can only suffer his whole life; he can only receive hurt everywhere. His life will be full of wounds and yet more wounds. Ego is comparing yourself with others; ego is ideas such as "I am superior to others."

Taking a pride in oneself is altogether a different thing. To take a pride in oneself is to be very humble. There is not even a question of being superior to others – everyone is unique in his own right. This is the understanding that goes with taking a pride in oneself: that nobody is higher than anyone else nor is anyone lower than anyone else. In this existence a small grass flower and the greatest star in the sky both have the same value. If even this small grass flower were missing, something would be missing in the whole existence that even the greatest star could not make up for.

Taking a pride in yourself is accepting the reality that everyone is unique and there is no race, no competition, no ambition. Yes, if someone is aggressive toward you, because taking a pride in yourself has no aggression in it, it will give you the capacity to fight back – but not to belittle the other, only to prove that the aggression of the other was wrong, that *all* aggression is wrong.

Taking a pride in yourself has no conceit: it is very simple and plain. But even the greatest power in the world cannot defeat a person who takes a pride in himself. This is a very unique mystery. Such a person is humble, so humble that by his own choice he will stand last in the queue. And so where else can he be pushed?

There is a particular episode in Abraham Lincoln's life. He was invited to a special conference of scientists. He went, but people were waiting for him at the door near the dais, because of course, the president of the country was coming, so the highest place on the dais had been reserved for him. But he came in through the same door through which the throngs of ordinary people were entering – people who had no name, no fame, no status – and he took a seat at the very back.

It started getting late for the meeting to begin. The organizers announced: "We are in a little difficulty. We have invited our president, Abraham Lincoln, but he has not yet arrived. And to begin the conference without him would be disgraceful, and it is getting late...."

The person sitting next to Abraham Lincoln nudged him and said, "Sir, why don't you stand up and announce that you are present and the conference can begin?"

Abraham Lincoln said, "I wanted it to be a quiet affair. It is a conference of scientists. What question is there of me being the center of it?"

But by this time others had also noticed him. The organizers came running up and said, "What are you doing, sir? This is not a blessing, but a disgrace upon our conference, that you should sit at the back."

Abraham Lincoln answered, "No. I am only sitting from where I cannot be pushed back any further."

This statement that "I am only sitting from where I cannot be pushed back any further" is the statement of a man who really takes a pride in himself. Such a man does not want to disgrace anyone, but he also does not give anyone the chance to disgrace him. Pride in oneself is a very simple matter.

The disease of ego is commonplace. The health of taking pride in oneself is rare, and when it is born in someone it is difficult to even recognize it, because it makes no claim. But the miracle is that this very "no claim" of pride in oneself becomes its very claim. A man who takes pride in himself never wants to hold himself above anyone, and he will never allow anyone else to impose any slavery upon him. Hence it can seem a little complex, and misinterpretations can happen.

Because of this misunderstanding, there have been a tremendously adverse effects upon India. For two thousand years we have remained slaves. What was the cause of our slavery? India is the only country in the history of the whole world that has never attacked anybody, because for centuries the seers, the sages, the enlightened ones of this country taught people only one thing: non-aggression, nonviolence, compassion, love. But this teaching remained somewhat incomplete. India understood the point that it should not attack, but it could not see that attack upon itself should also not be allowed. Because of this missing part, we remained slaves for two thousand years. India learnt that it should not commit violence, but it completely forgot that violence toward itself should also not be allowed. What difference does it make whether I commit violence to someone or I allow someone to commit violence to me? In both the cases I am allowing violence to take place.

Had this been understood rightly, this country would not have been in slavery for two thousand years. And still it has not been understood. We are still weighed down by those same old traditions and old ideas.

Whatever higher life experiences and discoveries are made, it is like walking on a razor's edge – walking very, very carefully. A slight mistake and...neither leaning to the left nor leaning to the right, but walking exactly in the middle. And so is the case with taking pride in oneself: neither does a person leave the impression of his ego on someone else nor does he give that person the right to leave the impression of their ego on him.

Hence, to be a man who takes a pride in himself is a spiritual process. To be an egoist is a worldly disease. In the Sanskrit word *swabhiman* – pride in oneself or self-respect – there is actually not a place for self or for pride. This is the difficulty of language, that there were words available to express the rubbish, but there were no words available to express the diamonds. So, we have had to create new words.

Abhiman, conceit, exactly represents the state of the egoist, but *swabhiman*? It became a dangerous word because half of it is *abhiman*, and there is fear you may define *swabhiman* by *abhiman*; you may take *abhiman* as *swabhiman*. But we have joined *swa*, self, to it – although the fear remains that *swa* can be given connotations of the ego too.

Those who joined *swa* to it did so with great consideration, and it did not have a question mark for them. Those who have joined *swa* to it, their meaning is that only he who has realized and who has known the *swa*, the self, has *swabhiman* – pride in himself or self-respect. Such a man can never have conceit, *abhiman*. And such a man can also never allow anyone else the opportunity to impose his *abhiman*, his pride, over him. Neither will he commit the offense nor will he allow anyone else to commit it.

But these are the weaknesses of language. *Abhiman*, conceit, is not an agreeable word, and even with the word *swa* the danger still remains that you may define it by ego. Ordinarily, there is no

59

difference between *swabhiman*, self-pride, and *abhiman*, conceit or ego. By ordinarily, I mean in *your* minds. The only difference is that you label your ego as taking a pride in yourself, and you call the other's taking a pride in himself, ego. This is the only difference.

But if you have recognized what I am saying... It certainly is subtle, but not so much so that it is impossible to understand.

CHAPTER 5

FORFEITING
DUALITY

Osho,
When does catharsis take place in the discipline of
Vipassana? I practice Vipassana. Also, in what way can
my work as a musician be helpful to me in moving
toward awareness?

Vipassana is a technique of meditation that is centuries old. It must
have been discovered thousands of years ago; who discovered it is not
known. It is an amazing technique. It is the easiest way to know oneself. The meaning of the word *vipassana* is: sitting silently becoming
a witness to oneself. *Pashya* means to see. *Vipassana* means sitting
silently within and seeing: here comes the "in" breath, here goes the
"out" breath – and to witness that also. The heart is beating – and
seeing that also. Sitting silently within, watching all that is happening
– just watching and witnessing – all sounds disappear and a great
nothingness surrounds you.

Buddha spread the technique of Vipassana worldwide, but there
exists one obstacle. And that obstacle is that twenty-five centuries
have gone by since Gautam Buddha's time, but the technique of
Vipassana has remained the same, although man's stupidity is no
longer the same. Man has kept moving from stupidity to even more
stupidity. Vipassana is a simple matter for any innocent person, but
modern man is not innocent. Modern man is so full of noise and so full
of dishonesties that you can forget all about being honest with others
– he is not even honest with himself.

I have heard:

A thief went on a pilgrimage with Eknath. Eknath was embarking on a pilgrimage and a whole group of his disciples was also going with him. This was a well-known thief – the whole village knew him. The thief asked Eknath to take him along on the pilgrimage too. "Save a poor wretch like me too! Let me also have the opportunity of visiting all the holy places with you," he said.

Eknath replied, "I have no objection, but there is one condition. The pilgrimage will last for three to six months and during that period you will not steal. Otherwise I don't want to bring you along if you will just be trouble. There will be fifty to sixty of my disciples and if you are stealing from them…"

The man said, "I swear to you that I will not steal."

Eknath consented, "Then there is no problem; you can come along."

But trouble started from the very second night. And the trouble was very strange. Somebody's bangles would end up on someone else's hand, somebody's ring had would end up on someone else's finger, somebody's items of the bedding would end up on someone else's bed. People were very puzzled when they woke up in the morning to see this strange phenomenon. The things would all be found – nothing was lost or stolen – but half the day would be wasted in just sorting out everybody's missing items. Someone would be saying, "Where are my spectacles?" Someone would be unable to find his money purse and would be searching for it. Until all the belongings of fifty or sixty people had been looked for: this money can't be found, these glasses can't be found…

Finally, after two nights, Eknath had to keep a vigil during the whole night. He had suspected the hand of the thief in all of this, and so it was. As everyone fell asleep, the thief would get up and start mixing up people's items.

Eknath said, "Foolish man! You had sworn not to steal."

The man said, "I had sworn not to steal, and that, I am not doing! But I had never sworn not to mix up people's things. Your pilgrimage will come to an end in three months, but this is my lifelong habit. And when everybody goes to sleep, that is when the day begins for me.

What am I supposed to do then, for all those long night hours? And I am not destroying anything of anybody's; I have not taken a single paise from anybody."

Habit! One is not to steal, but mixing things around – at least one derives some joy. The next morning he would be the only man who was sitting and joyously watching the whole scene that was going on around.

I have heard about such thieves who would steal from one of their own pockets and put the thing into another. This at least gives a little solace to their minds. They have saved face. It is a question of their prestige.

In these twenty-five centuries, so much perverted thought, so much suppression, so many clouds have covered man's mind that now it is very difficult to do Vipassana directly. And you are asking, "When does catharsis take place in Vipassana?" There is just no place for catharsis in Vipassana, because there was no need for catharsis in the days when Vipassana was invented. If there is simply no cancer, then what is the need for a treatment for it?

That's why I insist that my sannyasins do Dynamic Meditation before trying Vipassana, so that they can throw out all the rubbish during Dynamic Meditation, so that they become small children once again before starting Vipassana. But if you start Vipassana directly, you will create a dangerous situation: that which is suppressed within you will remain suppressed. Superficially you will appear peaceful but inside all that restlessness will go on accumulating. And that restlessness can one day burst forth like an explosion – it will. There is a limit to what you can keep suppressed.

I am not in favor of starting Vipassana directly; now Vipassana is the second step. Two thousand years ago it was the first step. Now, the first step is Dynamic Meditation. Dynamic Meditation will prepare you for Vipassana. Dynamic Meditation is not enough, you will not attain to enlightenment through it, but it will wash you clean as if you have just come out of the Ganges after taking a bath. To enter Vipassana in those moments of cleanliness is right; otherwise there is a danger.

But the greatest difficulty is that when thousands of years pass, people hold onto the past so emphatically that they forget the reality: that that past had been created for some other kind of people, not for you.

So the teachers of Vipassana are still teaching Vipassana without any idea of all that man has gone through in the meanwhile. Storms have passed over him, strong winds have passed over him. So much junk has gathered in him, so much rubbish has accumulated in him, that first it is necessary to clean that out.

So my suggestion is: make Dynamic Meditation your first step. And when you discover that there is nothing more within you to be thrown out, then start Vipassana. Then Vipassana itself will take you toward enlightenment.

The second thing is that you are a musician and you have asked how to practice music with awareness, or how to develop awareness and music together.

This is a little complex because when you are lost in music, you will forget awareness. When you are absorbed in music, who will be left there to become aware? And when you become aware, the music will be fragmented. So in an effort to harmonize two opposing things, you will fall into difficulty. There will be a tremendous push and pull.

Just choose any one of the two and that's enough. It is not good to board two boats simultaneously; it is of no help to ride two horses simultaneously. You may try it in a million ways, but the danger is unavoidable.

Music is enough; just drown totally. Drown so totally that there remains no awareness in you that there is a musician: only the music remains. And the doors of the eternal will open.

There are many doors to existence. It is very fortunate that there is not just one door, otherwise there would be such a crowd there. And that would be difficult: queues would form, queues that will last for centuries; buddhas will have to wait for centuries at the gate. But existence has an endless number of doors: music is enough.

If one wants to practice awareness, then music cannot be taken to its ultimate depths. You can make music an object for awakening, you can keep awareness over your music, but that awareness will not be able to take the music to its heights or to its depths.

In the West there was a great dancer, Nijinsky. There has probably never been any other such wondrous dancer as he was in the whole history of mankind. A specialty of Nijinsky's dancing was that while dancing he would take leaps of such height that they went against the laws of gravity. Even those who practice the high jump for the Olympics couldn't take those kinds of leaps. And Nijinsky was not a practitioner of the high jump, but while he was dancing, moments would come when it was "as if he had grown wings." He used to take such high leaps that scientists were astonished; such leaps are not ordinarily possible with the gravitation of the earth.

And the matter didn't end there. The matter would become even more astonishing when he started coming down from the jump. The earth pulls falling things down with tremendous force, and they gain great speeds, up to six thousand miles a minute. When you see shooting stars in the night…

And by the way, no star is shooting; stars are very big things. If they were "falling" we would have fallen apart long ago. No, no star falls. When the earth separated from the sun and the moon was formed out of the earth, in those volatile times, many smaller objects called meteorites also formed that are now scattered around the earth and revolve around it. Whenever a meteorite falls within the earth's gravitational sphere – which is two hundred miles around it – the earth pulls it with tremendous force. The falling meteorite goes on gaining speed, up to six thousand miles a minute, and because of the great friction that is generated between the meteorite and the atmosphere, the meteorite turns into a glowing fire. It is not a star; it is burning matter called a meteorite.

So when Nijinsky came down from his leap, he would come floating down like the feather of a bird – in no hurry. This was an even bigger surprise, his coming down was a bigger surprise because it defied the gravitational law of the earth completely.

People used to ask Nijinsky how he managed this. Nijinsky would say, "Don't ask how I do it. Whenever I try to do it, it never happens. I tried this at home and it never happens; I have tried this on stage too and it never happens. When I am tired of trying and forget all about it, then one day, suddenly, I find it has happened. But this happens when I am not, when my effort is not there, when I am not trying, when I am not making an endeavor, when my desire is not there, when my lust is not there. This is as much a mystery to me as it is to you. When I have disappeared, then this phenomenon takes place."

This is also the experience of great painters. Only when they disappear do their hands turn into the hands of existence. This is also the experience of great musicians. When they are no more there, some other power, some supreme power, starts arranging the music on their instrument.

So if you are a musician and you love music, don't worry about awareness. Worry about drowning into the music so that only music remains and you are not. You will reach exactly the same place where those who practiced supreme awareness have reached. There, too, the same thing is being done: one has to forget oneself in supreme awareness. In the beginning the person is there. The abc of awareness is initiated by the person, but the final alphabet is not written by the person. It is written by the hands of the impersonal that resides within us all – the formless that is within us all.

It doesn't make any difference from which door you attain to nothingness. All doors belong to it. Use whichever door you love, because ultimately it is your love that will be able to take you to the depths – to the depths where you become willing to disappear. Nothing other than love can ever make you willing to disappear.

So it is good, it is fortunate that you are a musician. Drown into music. Let only music remain and you will reach. You will not even notice when you arrive. It is only upon reaching that you will realize, "Oh, where am I? Only godliness is! Where am I? Only existence is!"

But to ride two horses simultaneously is dangerous. And in spiritual life, many people unknowingly start riding several horses at the same time. They reach nowhere. They only fracture their limbs and end up in some hospital. One horse is enough. In order to attain to one, one alone is enough. The duality has to be forfeited, and you are trying to ride the duality.

CHAPTER 6

PICKING UP THE
DIAMONDS

Osho,
From Morarji Desai's government through to Rajiv Gandhi's,
you have only ever been a critic. Do you, however, have
a particular viewpoint or answer of your own for
solving the problems of this country?

The problems of this country are bigger than this country itself. And my criticism is not negative. It is a positive approach toward solving these problems.

For example, when a surgeon operates on someone's cancer, would you call the operation negative? It appears to be negative, but in reality it is positive. And before an old building is demolished and a new building can be raised, it is necessary to make people alert that it is dangerous to live in that old building, it can destroy life.

I have never criticized anybody in my whole life, but this is a fact that cannot be helped: that when there is a thorn stuck in someone's foot it has to be prised out with another thorn. That other thorn is not an enemy, it is a friend – although it too is a thorn.

So the first thing that I want to make very clear is that I am not a critic. My viewpoint is creative, but before creating, demolition is a must. And thousands of years of old rotten traditions, superstitions, that are heavy on our backs and do not allow this country to move ahead…as long as we do not get rid of them, no positive, no creative reconstruction is possible.

The problems are so many that they cannot even be counted. Here I will discuss only the basic ones. But remember, it is not criticism, it is not negative. I do not believe in "no." I call "yes" religiousness.

The first challenge facing this country is to free itself from its past. And your politicians cannot do it, because the politician has to beg for votes from the very people whose past it is. Understand it this way: when a child is born, it has only the future and no past. When it is a youth, it has the present. When it is old, it has only a past. A country that has only a past has become old. It is on its deathbed; it will be in the coffin any day.

For example, Mahatma Gandhi, wanted no railway trains, no telephones, no telegraph, no electricity, no machines...no dimensions of technology in this country. For him, the progress of the world stopped at the spinning wheel. But this human race cannot survive with just the spinning wheel. If a man were to work only on the spinning wheel every day, eight hours a day continuously spinning yarn, then he could create clothes just for himself for the whole year – nothing for his wife, nothing for his children, nothing for his parents. But you cannot eat clothes, you cannot drink clothes. And if for eight hours a day you were only to spin a wheel, you would be the greatest dimwit. From where would you get your food? From where would you get clothes for your wife and children? How would you build your house? Hence, I have made the observation that until this country becomes free of Mahatma Gandhi's noose, it has no future.

The world has made a tremendous leap forward. A small machine can do more work than one thousand people. And the special thing about a machine is that it doesn't get tired. It doesn't have to change shifts. It can go on working around the clock. And the even more special thing about a machine is that it doesn't die. If any part stops functioning, it can be replaced.

But Gandhi was stubborn. And his disciples in whose hands this country has remained for the forty years since Independence don't even have enough guts to admit that now that Gandhi himself is gone, it is essential to say goodbye to this childish vision of his as well.

The first thing is that this country has to be developed with the greatest, newest technology and technical knowledge – which is not difficult, which is very easy. But the dilemma is that if Mahatma

Gandhi is worshipped then it is very difficult to bring technology into this country.

When Gandhi died, the population of this country was already four hundred million. This population situation has only gone on worsening day by day. But even with this emergency situation, no mother's son dares to make it clear to the nation that you cannot control the population of this country through celibacy.

On one side there is a lack of technology which is like having your hands tied, and on the other side is the population explosion, which is a harbinger of death. Those who are specialists in population growth and calculations have had the idea that by the end of this century the population of India will be one billion. But the latest research says that it will be 1.8 billion, not just one billion. In a country that has already been suffering hunger and difficulty from having a population of four hundred million, you can very well imagine that a population of 1.8 billion will be an open invitation to death. But the politician cannot say this. Even if he knows about it, he cannot say it. A politician has to cover himself with masks – mask upon mask upon mask – because, he cannot touch any of the beliefs of the people from whom he has to get votes.

For centuries India has believed that children are gifts from God. Now, this concept has to be dropped. Children are your own doing, not the gift of any god. Just think: if children were gifts of God, of his grace and love, then the growing population would have been filled life with more love, with more friendliness and bliss. Only two conclusions can be drawn: either your God is a devil...

And also your God is omniscient! He knows the past, present and the future, and yet he cannot see that with a population of 1.8 billion people the roads will be covered with corpses! There won't even be enough people to carry the dead bodies to the crematorium. It will be impossible to arrange even shrouds for the corpses, because if, in line with Gandhism, the spinning wheel continues, there will be no possibility even to produce enough shrouds.

So the first thing I want to say is that India has to become free of its past and has to focus its sights toward the future. If God or nature had had such an attachment to the past, it would have given you eyes in the back of your skull – not in the front – so that you could look backward. It has given you eyes in the front.

Why are political thinkers unable to gather the courage to say that there should be birth control in this country? A fear, a dread. The public believes that children are gifts of God, so a politician who insists on birth control is not going to get their votes. Hence everyone may see the situation but they are all keeping quiet.

There should be compulsory birth control in India for at least thirty years. After all, what is the point of bringing children into the world whom you will neither be able to feed, nor clothe, for whom you cannot provide an education, and if they fall sick, you won't be able to provide any medicine.

But the Mohammedan looks towards the Koran. Mohammed married nine women, so he gave every Mohammedan the right, the dignity, to marry at least four women. This is worth understanding. If a woman has nine husbands, there is no problem, because she will be able to give birth to only one child each year. But, if a man has nine women, there is a danger. He can produce nine children every year. And the Mohammedans insist that it is their religious law.

But Mohammed did not give a place to this edict in the Koran for any spiritual reason. Mohammed's whole life passed carrying a naked sword in his hands. Naturally, the men used to die in wars and the women would remain. The natural balance was disturbed. There were four times more women than men, and if the rule of one man marrying one woman had continued, what was going to happen to the remaining three women? Education was out of question; they could not even raise their veils. These three women were bound to become prostitutes, so it was better that every man should be allowed the concession of marrying four women.

However, when you allow concessions, strange dangers arise.

Just this century, when India became independent, the Nizam of Hyderabad had five hundred wives – although the proportion of men to women in the world is equal. And when one man takes possession of five hundred women, what are the remaining four hundred and ninety-nine men, without women, going to do? Perversion is bound to spread. Immorality and corruption are bound to take root.

But don't be too angry with the Nizam. The one who broke all records in the world is the perfect incarnation of godliness, Krishna. He had sixteen thousand women. And amongst these sixteen thousand women, only one, Rukmini, was his married wife. All others were the wives of other people. Any woman he liked was immediately taken to his palace. There is an English saying: "Might is right." Krishna had the might. If he took some poor man's wife, the man could not even say no. That woman might have had small children, might have had a husband or elderly people in the family. Those houses were left deserted, destroyed. Those houses became engulfed in darkness. And yet you go on calling Krishna a perfect incarnation of godliness – this man who didn't even possess a simple humanity! Being a perfect incarnation is a far cry from this.

The first thing is: India has to become free of its past. Then, we can take new steps.

The first of the new steps will be birth control. And in this rotten world where man does nothing except murder – man has fought five thousand wars in three thousand years, and now he is preparing for the last war – if you have any love, you will not want to bring your child into this world.

If India can observe total birth control for thirty years, its population will come down to the point where we can become prosperous.

I can say this to you because I am not a politician and I don't have to ask for votes from you. Yes, if you want you can stone me; I will take that as a blessing. But the politician is in business. He has to say what you like to hear. And your likings are very rotten, very old, very decayed. You have never even reexamined them.

In the times of Gautam Buddha, the population of the whole world was only twenty million – the population of the whole world! And if people were prosperous and if people did not use locks on their houses, it is understandable. Why lock them? There was so much prosperity – particularly in this country, which is more like a continent than a country. All the different seasons are here, all sorts of natural resources are here. You can find the coldest of places and you can also find the hottest of places here. There are dry deserts, and there are places like Cherapoonji, where the annual rainfall is five hundred inches, where you cannot even go out of your house.

India is a whole world in itself. It was affluent beyond calculation. Those people who called it a "golden bird" were not wrong. People were happy; people were joyous. There came a metaphor that rivers of milk and honey flowed here. No rivers of milk and honey flowed, but this expression is indicative of the fact that things were so plentiful that even if we had made rivers of milk and honey flow, there would have been no harm, no problem. The basic facts behind this were a small population and a big country; a big land, a fertile land.

If the destiny of this country is to be given a golden glow again, if the stones of this country are to be polished into diamonds again, we will have to show some courage. The interesting thing, however, is that the Christian priests, cardinals or popes come to this country and explain to people that birth control is a sin. And the *shankaracharyas* and the *jainacharyas* of this country are in agreement with them – although their concern is somewhere else. The Christian wants this country to go on becoming poorer and poorer because the more poor people there are, the more people will convert to Christianity – they are bound to. And the shankaracharyas and the jainacharyas are afraid that if it goes on like this, their numbers will diminish. This country could become a Christian country tomorrow, so produce more children!

So, the first thing I want to say is that if you love children, do not produce any. For just thirty years observe birth control. Those who have wanted to reduce the population, like Mahatma Gandhi, like Vinoba Bhave, were also against birth control. They would say, "Observe celibacy." And can anyone give any figures on how many people Mahatma Gandhi turned into celibates? Mahatma Gandhi's own personal secretary ran away with a girl.

Celibacy is unnatural. And with the work that a small pill can do, standing unnecessarily on your head doing *shirshasana* is utter stupidity. No matter how much you try, you cannot go against the laws of nature unless you take support from science – and the full support of science is available today. Up until very recently, the pill was only available for women. Today, we have it for men too.

The population of this country is the enemy, the problem of this country. It can be solved very easily; just a little intelligence.

Five thousand sannyasins were living in the commune that I had created in America – two and a half thousand pairs of men and women. But in five years not a single child was born there. No guns were used to make this happen, nor had any police to enforce it. Just a little explaining.

The second thing: India has been in slavery for two thousand years: sometimes under the Moghuls, sometimes under the Turks, sometimes under the Hoonas, sometimes under Mohammedans, sometimes under the English. Two thousand years is a long time. This slavery of two thousand years has settled in your minds so deeply that it doesn't want to leave you. This slavery must be dispelled from your minds, because it is not just about the slavery. This slavery has also brought a whole lot of other rubbish with it into your minds that will only go when this slave mentality disappears. Although you appear to have become free, it is just an appearance – no change has taken place to the inner slavery.

Slavery is a chain that inhibits man's intelligence.

In three hundred years the English created schools, colleges and universities in this country, but not so that you could be educated, but so that you could remain deprived of becoming educated. And they arranged the whole educational system in a way that these schools, colleges and universities became mere factories for producing clerks. Can you imagine that a vast country like India, which will be the biggest country in the world population-wise by the end of the twentieth century, has so far claimed only three Nobel Prizes? And the Jews, who are not so many in number – almost none in India – take forty percent of the Nobel Prizes every year.

What is the reason? Have our brains become completely empty, hollow? They have been made hollow, and very scientific methods of making them hollow have been used. Somebody is a Hindu, someone a Mohammedan, someone a Jaina, someone a Sikh, and the English always tried to ensure that this country would never unite; that it kept on fighting within itself; that all its energies went to waste in fighting with each other. Their first act in this was via Jinnah, who never even went to jail, who never faced any police crackdown during the Freedom Struggle. And yet he became the cause of this country being divided into three parts, because the English had filled this country's mind very deeply with one thing, which had never been there before.

If you look at the holy book of the Sikhs, the *Guru Granth*, there are words of the Hindu mystics there, there are words of the Mohammedan fakirs like Farid there. Until this time our dedication was to truth. In one single book, the *Guru Granth*, the words of people from all religions who have spoken truth are compiled. But the English slowly raised walls amongst them.

Before the Indian Independence, Winston Churchill had said – at that point he was not the prime minister – that Attlee was making a mistake: "India's freedom would divide it into pieces, and its independence would become a chaos." And no matter what a charlatan Churchill may have been in politics, this statement of his was true. In the name of independence what came was peril. Hundreds of millions of people became homeless, their wives were raped, and thousands got burned and butchered. And this was Mahatma Gandhi's long teaching in nonviolence that finally culminated in violence – not only in violence within the country, but Gandhi himself was shot by a Hindu.

So, I would like only human beings to live in this country. Hindu, Mohammedan, Christian and Sikh – these are your own personal and private matters. You go to the *gurudwara*, that is what you like; you go to a mosque, that is what you like – but where is the fight in it? You read the Koran, that is what you like. You take an interest in the Gita or immerse yourself in the Upanishads – what is the problem in it, where is the fight about it?

At least the youth of this country should understand that they are only human beings. Firstly they are human beings, and only then whatsoever else they may be. All the rest is their own private matters, like what brand of cigarettes you smoke – but there is never any fight about that – or which film star you are a fan of – that is up to you.

Religion is a completely personal and private matter. It has nothing to do with a group. Where you receive juice from, where you receive life from, where you receive peace from is your *dwar*, your door. But do not drag others through that door as well.

Most of the energy of this country is spent in people fighting with each other. This same energy could fill this country with flourishing fields of crops, but instead it has been filling this country with blood. We haven't even worried about butchering those who are our own – were our own – and we have forgotten that we are human beings. We have behaved like animals.

My suggestions are very simple and straightforward.

Religion should be declared a personal matter. Religion should not be an organization. It should be everyone's freedom and what they like. And it is possible, too, that today you may enjoy going to a *gurudwara*, and tomorrow, reciting *ajaan* in a mosque may begin to fascinate you – and there is no harm in it. All are sacred – *gurudwaras*, mosques, temples and churches – and they are all ours. Wherever you can find diamonds, pick them up. And wherever you find even a small glimpse of the truth, absorb it. But instead of this, we are bloodthirsty toward each other.

It is a matter for the smallest of understanding.

Never ask anybody, "What is your religion?" There is only one religion: to make oneself one with this infinite universal consciousness. How you do it is your choice. Which path you tread, which ladder you climb is your choice. Never, even by mistake, say, "My religion." You can be of religion; religion can never be yours. Religion is not a thing that you can put your seal on, that you can put your signature on, that "this is my religion." And the day you do this – "this is my religion" – that day your ego naturally says that my religion is the only real religion.

No. *You* become religion; do not make the religion yours. People have climbed the Everest of religiousness from countless paths. You can choose the path you like. Even this much is not necessary: that your wife walks on your path, with you. And this too is not necessary: that your children walk on your path.

Religion is the ultimate freedom. There is no bigger freedom than religion. So it is possible that the wife may be going to a Jaina temple, the husband may be going to the *gurudwara*, and the children may be doing namaaz in a mosque. This will be a very lovely thing. If in one single house there are people practicing all religions, the fights over religion that unnecessarily waste and turn our energy and creative power to dust can be abolished from this country.

I would also like to say to you that you have been taught for centuries that there is some spirituality in poverty. If there was spirituality in poverty we would not have called the ultimate reality *Ishwar*, God. *Ishwar* means affluence, opulence. It is the ultimate richness. Do you think that if you met Ishwar someday, he will be standing naked in the hot sun, or will be lying down on a bed of thorns? Religion is not poverty. Religion is the ultimate affluence of life, both outer and inner. And there is no contradiction between the two. To meditate sitting in a desert or to meditate sitting in the peace and quietness of your own house...I would ask you to choose the house, because meditation will be difficult in the desert. The peace of your house will give you more silence.

We have also been told that a religious person should renounce the world. He escapes – to the mountains, to the caves, to the desert. This has had ill effects. The ill effects are that hundreds of millions of escapists have been running away from the world for centuries. They have left their wives, children, old parents, widowed sisters, without a thought of what will happen to them. These children will become beggars, and only tomorrow or the day after Mother Teresa will turn them into Christians. These millions of monks who have run away from their homes are escapists. What will happen to their wives? Either they will have to become beggars or prostitutes. Both things are ugly.

I want to say to you that religion is not an escape from the world. Religion is to beautify the world. On the one hand you say that God created the world, and on the other, your saints and monks ask you to renounce the world. The arithmetic is clear: your saints are against God. If the world is meant to be renounced like that, what was the necessity of creating it in the first place? And if being in the world is in itself a sin, then the whole responsibility goes to God, not to you. And if anybody goes to hell, it will be your God, because it is he who created the world, he who gave you desires and passions. You are completely innocent. You are only a puppet in his hands. If someone has to be punished, it should be God.

George Gurdjieff was one of the most significant persons of this century. He literally made this statement, that "all the saints and monks are against God." When I read it for the first time, it shocked me. What is this man saying? But when I understood it, I discovered that this man was saying the right thing. They teach you that God creates the world, saints and monks urge you to renounce it – they are clearly against God.

If you have to choose one of the two, choose God. Make the world more beautiful. You should leave the world more beautiful than you have found it when you were born – then you have done some service to existence. No matter whether you went to any temple or not – that makes no difference – but you have grown a few new flowers in the temple of existence, you have brought a little more fragrance into this world, you have made an offering of your life's intelligence to existence.

It is not very difficult to transform this country. This country can be given back its former glory within ten years, because this country has not lost its genius. Only ash has gathered on its embers, which must be blown away.

Osho,
How will your journey toward the unknowable proceed?
Would you like to establish some new schools and communes?

No. The communes and the schools that I established were only experiments to find out if what I was saying could become a reality or not. Could these dreams be actualized or not?

I witnessed those dreams being actualized. Now I would like this whole world to become my commune; for the whole world to enter the mystery, this world of wonder for which we were born and which is our destiny.

So now, individual communes and schools…those were the first experiments. They have succeeded. From them I have obtained keys for how this whole world can be transformed. If I only go on creating schools and communes, this will be a very trivial thing. Why not transform this whole world into a university where every person can make a journey into the mystery, and every person can move toward the unknowable? Now I want to make the whole world my commune. Now I have the exact keys, which I have tested on the right touchstone – that they are pure, twenty-four carat gold.

I remember: I was in Greece, staying on a small island of Greece. Thousands of sannyasins from all over Europe had gathered in the gardens of that house. But the tree under which I was sitting…

I had never seen that kind of tree before. I asked, "What is the name of this tree?" And I was surprised when I was told that in Greek it is called *carob* – and it is a tree that is unique in this whole world, because each of its small beans is of the exact same weight. The beans of the carob – no matter where they grow – there is no difference in their weight. This carob has become carat in the other languages, and there was no better way in the past than to use the carob beans to weigh gold. The carob never deceives; its weight is always the same.

That is why we say "twenty-four carat gold." That use of carat has been born out of this unique feature of the carob beans: that their weight is always the same no matter which country they grow in, what climate they grow in.

I have tested those keys for transformation to twenty-four carat accuracy. Naturally, small communes and small schools were necessary to test them. All human beings are similar. The color of their skin may be different, that makes no difference whatsoever. Their height and their build may be different, that makes no difference whatsoever. But within them, within every man, there is twenty-four

81

carat gold. And now I would like that these same keys are made available to the whole world. Why should only India grow affluent with these keys? Why should only India become magnificent and not the whole of humanity?

This approach of mine, that I take the whole of humanity as one family and take every human being as a human being, puts me in a very strange situation. The religions of the whole world and the politicians of the whole world have conspired together not to let me work – because the Christian is afraid that if a Christian hears my words he will become a human being, but he will no longer remain a Christian; and the Hindu is afraid that if a Hindu hears my words he will become a human being, but he will no longer remain a Hindu.

Now a single individual, ready to give the keys of transformation to the whole world… And naturally the world is divided into so many fragments. There are three hundred religions in the world, and each religion thinks it is the only true religion, that all the others are insubstantial. And I am saying that man is the reality, his humanness is the reality, and it is within his humanness that godliness resides. Whichever scripture he reads, whichever temple he visits, that is according to his liking, it is his recreation.

Perhaps it may have never happened before: that the whole world is against a single individual. But I take it as a compliment, because whenever the whole world is against one single individual, then one thing is certain: that the whole world cannot be right. If it were, the world today would have been a different place altogether. And the whole world being in opposition to one single man is proof of the fact that the journey to my victory has begun. They have already accepted their defeat inwardly; now they are just making an effort to cover it up.

Osho,
Will Rajneeshism – your movement – once again influence the world so startlingly, or will you simply end up as yet another Charvaka, the propagator of the "eat, drink and be merry" philosophy?

There are two questions within this one question.

First, will Rajneeshism once again influence the world so startlingly?

Neither has there ever been such a thing as "Rajneeshism" nor will there ever be. I am an enemy of "isms." It is these "isms" which have destroyed the world. After all, what is Christianity? After all, what is Mohammedanism? After all, what is Jainism? These are the attempts of certain individuals to take the whole world under their influence. They have all failed. And in that failure, they have thrown the whole world into such a mess.

I am not ready to commit any such sin. I do not want to bring the world under my influence. I would like the world to take me under its influence: for it to forget my name, forget my address, and remember itself. I do not want to leave any religion behind me.

I have only one request to those people who love me, for there to be only one proof of their love: that they forgive me and forget me forever. Yes, if any truth has manifested through me, then just drink that truth – drink it to your heart's content. But the truth is not mine; it is nobody's. Truth is only its own. There is no label on it, no adjective to it.

Hence, I want to just melt, merge, disappear, in such a way that not even any trace of my footprints is left on the earth so that someone may follow them. In the same way that birds fly in the sky yet leave no trace behind, I also don't want to leave any footprints behind me.

I want humanity to love truth, to love love, to love compassion, to love meditation, to love existence itself – to love all *these* things. I was not here yesterday; tomorrow again I will not be here. Do not turn this skeleton into a statue.

And I don't want to take anybody under my influence.

In regard to this let me also tell you that the people in this world who make the effort to gather followers so that people can fall under their influence are not good people. They are egoists. They want to take the peak of their ego higher and higher. They want to stand on your shoulders and touch the stars in the sky.

I want to disappear in such a way that it is as if I never existed.

And only that will remain which has always been, which always was and which always will be – and that you remain under the influence of this. What has anything got to do with me? What is my value?

The second part of your question: "Will you simply end up becoming yet another Charvaka?"

Perhaps you are not aware of the meaning of the word *charvaka*. And perhaps you are also not aware that there was never a person called Charvaka. Charvaka was a tradition, a philosophy of life. The people who were against that philosophy of life gave it the name Charvaka. The meaning of the word *charvaka* is: one who believes in eating and drinking: "Eat, drink and be merry. Go on feasting and enjoying!" But this is not the real name of that tradition either. The tradition's own name was Charu Vak – not Charvaka, but Charu Vak. And charu vak means "sweet words." *Charu* means sweet, *vak* means words.

It is so amazing to see what man has done to man. It is such dishonesty that they distorted the real name, the traditional name, which only indicated "Let there be a sweetness in life. Let flowers shower in your every word."

Certainly Charu Vak propagated that whatever life has been given to you, enjoy it to the fullest. The tradition of Charu Vak is not about renouncing, it is not an escape, it is not anti-life. The tradition of Charu Vak is to fill life with as much sweet nectar as possible – that is its wish.

You will be surprised to know that not a single scripture of the long tradition of Charu Vak is available. Hindus burned all the scriptures, because the very message was so sweet that there was danger. And its message was so reasonable, that the priest felt a danger. Charu Vak was saying, "Don't worry about the other world. If you have lived the joys of this world, in beauty and sweetness, then if there is any other world..." mark its words, "...if there is any other world, it can only be an extension of this world."

And its honesty was such that it said, "Until I die, how can I know that there is some other world, because so far no one has ever returned to tell us 'Yes, there is another world.' So, I can say only this much to you: that with as much love and bliss as you can live that which is, and as much as your life can become a dance, and as sweet as the sound of your ankle bells can become, the better. Because, if there is any other world, the foundations of that world will be laid in this world. After all, it is you who will be going to that other world. And if you are blissful here, you will be even more blissful there. And if there is no other world, then no question arises. Neither will you be there, nor will there be any experiences."

A sincere philosophical tradition.

But all your so-called religions live with the support of the "other world." They destroy your this world and give you assurances that you will be rewarded for it in the other world. And if you look at the rewards you will be puzzled.

Mohammedans say that a person who drinks wine in this world is the biggest sinner. But in their other world there are rivers of flowing wine. Do you see any logic in this? If you want to be a saint here, do not drink wine – don't even touch it, don't even pass near a pub. And it is only a question of a few days because Mohammedans, Christians and Jews believe in only one life – most has passed, only a little is left. This too will pass. Just manage somehow, and then the other world will come where there will be only bliss and more bliss.

Hindus monks say that if you love a woman here you will fall into hell. But, if you really want the love of the most beautiful celestial damsels, then just wait, just keep a little patience: the other world is full of these damsels.

And the description of them is also worth considering. Century after century has gone by – endless time has passed – but those damsels of the other world have always remained sixteen years of age. They do not age. It seems they are made of plastic, not of flesh. And this too is interesting, that they are not faithful to one man. Endless numbers of saints and monks have kept arriving and receiving the fruits of their virtues. And the most surprising thing is that here even to touch a woman is sin, and there it is a huge gathering of women awaiting the saints and the monks.

I see some logical error in all of this. If it is true that there are women waiting there, then at least allow for some rehearsal here.

Here, your saint or monk is withering and dying, has become nearly dead in his efforts to observe celibacy throughout his life. Now if celestial damsels surround this man he will run away. He will say, "Mother! What is this you do to me?"

I have heard that a great Hindu saint, whose whole teaching was that celibacy is the only way to attain to the ultimate reality, died. He was very much respected. After his death his closest disciple could not bear the separation and the very second day after the saint died, the disciple's heart also failed. He was on his way to the heaven, very happy that he would soon be seeing his guru.

When he arrived in heaven, he saw that the dry boned old man was lying naked under a tree and America's recently dead superstar actress Marilyn Monroe, whom President Kennedy also used to meet secretly, was embracing him – his guru! He thought, "Oh my God! Shall I keep my eyes open or shut? Of course, according to the scriptures, they should be shut, but my desire is to watch with open eyes."

And as every man may find some tricky way, he fell at the feet of his guru and said, "My master! I knew that having observed such strict celibacy, you would reap the greatest reward for it."

Before the guru could say anything, Marilyn Monroe said, "You fool! Your guru is not being rewarded. I am being punished! Who knows when this rotten man even took his last shower!"

This is the arrangement of all religions: Destroy this world so that in the other world, you can be rewarded. But this is absolutely against all logic, against all mathematics. If enjoyment is to be delivered to you in the other world, then it is essential that you have some practice of it here, in this world. This is just a small school where you can take some lessons, then in the other world...

Do not call Charu Vak "Charvaka"; call it "Charu Vak" – its words are very sweet. All its books were burnt, the tradition was completely destroyed, but some excerpts can be found in the books of its opponents who were quoting from it in order to destroy it.

Even those few excerpts are enough to show that the man who

started this tradition must have been of extreme genius. It unites the other world and this world. It is not dividing, it is not compartmentalizing life. It is making it one indivisible unit. And he is saying to you that this world belongs to existence, and the other world also belongs to existence; that the abyss of conflict should go.

You ask, "Will you simply end up as yet another Charvaka?"

Perhaps you are not aware of my whole philosophy of life. My whole philosophy of life is to bridge Charu Vak and Gautam Buddha. Gautam Buddha is the other world; Charu Vak is this world. Charu Vak is incomplete if it has no idea of the other world, and Gautam Buddha is incomplete if he is denying this life herenow.

I accept life in its wholeness. I am Charu Vak and I have touched the height of Buddhahood too – and I have not found any antagonism between the two. There simply cannot be any opposition within life because it is one organic unit. There is no "two" here. It is all an expansion of one existence. The feet of the divine are as essential as the head. Do not cut it into two parts otherwise the feet will die, and the head will also die.

I want to see both together. I want to see Buddha with all the bliss and all the potential of this life, and I want to see Charu Vak with all the heights of the other world.

Why can't this be done? I have seen this happen in myself, hence I say with authority that if it can happen within me, it can also happen within you.

To accept life as one single indivisible unit is the most significant aspect of man's genius.

CHAPTER 7

THE ULTIMATE
OPULENCE:
LOVE AND MEDITATION

THE DIAMOND SWORD

Osho,
I gain intellectual understanding through study, reflection and
listening, but my life goes on being hurt and manipulated by my
emotions, and shocks arising from my unconscious labyrinths.
I am helpless. So far I haven't had access to these unconscious
places. Could you give me some technique, some practice, a
thread or direction to follow?

What is gained through study, reflection and pondering is not even intellectual understanding. It is merely a fallacy of understanding. It is like explaining to a blind man about light. He listens to it, then there is a mode for teaching the blind so he also studies through that means, and then whatsoever he has listened to and studied, he may ponder and reflect over it. But do you think this will be *knowing* light? Yes, he may gain a false notion that he knows light, but that fallacy is even more dangerous than blindness itself – because if a blind man understands that he does not know light, there is a possibility he may search for some treatment to cure his eyes, but if he thinks that he already knows what light is then even that door is closed.

There are two parts to your question. You are saying that study, listening and reflection bring intellectual understanding. Neither has intellect ever understood anything nor will it ever. But you are blessed that you have the realization that this understanding is not helping you at all. Within you are deep darkness and unconscious desires – and you are aware of this reality. Even amidst all the commotion of your intellect, you have not completely forgotten their presence and the terrible mess they have created within you.

90

So one statement that you make about gaining intellectual understanding is incorrect, but your other statement is precious. And you are blessed that even in believing it to be understanding, you have not become "wise"; you have not taken that understanding to be your wisdom. There are many unfortunate people who waste their lives in that very "wisdom."

The reality is that you are much more than the intellect, you are far beyond the intellect. The function of the intellect is to know things which are alien to you; to know others who are not you. So the intellect is not your enemy. It is through the intellect that the whole of science has been born. But you can make the intellect your enemy if you start thinking that you can also come to know yourself through it.

Look at it like this. A person tries to hear music through his eyes, or someone else tries to see light through his ears. Neither the eyes nor the ears are at fault in this. The eyes are for seeing light, not for hearing music. The ears are for hearing music, not for seeing light.

The function of the intellect is to know things, to know that which is other than you. But the function of the intellect is not to know the knower. The knower sitting within you is not a thing, and that is why science is in great difficulty. Science knows so much about so many stars, knows so much about atoms and sub-atoms, but the scientist misses knowing himself. He knows everything but misses knowing the one who knows all this.

And in general it appears natural to think that through that by which we have known everything else, we can also come to know the knower. You can see the whole world through your eyes, but you cannot see your own eyes. It is a different matter to go and stand in front of a mirror, but what you will see is not your eyes, only a reflection of them, an image of them. What helplessness! Eyes see everything but are unable to see themselves.

It is a similar situation.

You have asked, "How may I fill my unconscious, my darkness with light?" You will have to do a small thing, a very small thing. Twenty-four hours – day, and night also – you are busy seeing others. At least for a little while, engage yourself in forgetting the other. The day you forget the other completely, the use of the intellect will no longer be there. This, the mystics have called meditation.

Meditation means a state where nothing remains to be known, where only the knower remains. There is no way to get rid of the knower. No matter how much you escape – to the mountains, to the deserts, to the moon and the stars – the knower in you will always be with you, because it is you. It is your innermost being. You cannot run away, leaving it behind. It is not a reflection. It is your very existence.

Every day, start giving an hour in the morning, or in the evening, or at noon, to this unique dimension. Just sit with closed eyes.

But you have developed bad habits, and there are professionals who take advantage of your bad habits. They say, "Close your eyes and see how Lord Krishna is playing on his flute! See how Jesus is hanging on the cross! Close your eyes and see this couple called Rama and Sita." But then you are still entangled with others, even with closed eyes. Your eyes have closed, but you cannot rid yourself of the other.

There is a unique statement of Gautam Buddha: "Even if I appear before you on the path of meditation, take up a sword and cut me in two pieces. If you are my disciple and you have understood what I have been saying, then do not hesitate even for a moment – because even the master appearing on the path of meditation is the other."

Perhaps that is the last of all struggles. To renounce your wife is not such a big thing. Those who have renounced their wives have escaped to the forests, have taken sannyas, have become great seekers and great monks. Probably you think that they have accomplished an almost impossible task. You are hugely mistaken. You are accomplishing the impossible task in still being with your wife! Those who have run away are escapists. But such escapism, such running away, is not going to solve anything.

If you run away from wealth, that too is not going to make any difference. The desire for wealth is going to follow you. There is no sin in wealth; the sin comes in craving wealth and where will you leave your craving? If there was any sin in wealth, then thieves deserve rewards, not punishment. What great pains the poor fellows take to relieve others of their sin! If there was any virtue in renouncing your wife, then the person who has run away with someone's wife deserves paradise.

I have heard...

A man came running to the post office. He was perspiring profusely from the effort. The postmaster sat him down and asked what the problem was.

The man said, "Please, lodge a report in my name. My wife has run away with someone."

The postmaster said, "I fully sympathize with you and I understand that in the panic of the situation you forgot that this is a post office, not the police station. The police station is opposite here."

The man said, "I know that – but please, register the report."

The post master said, "You are a strange fellow. This is not the work of a post office. This is a task for the police station. You will have to get your report lodged there."

The man said, "I did that once before and the idiots located her and brought her back the very next day. I am not going to repeat the same mistake again."

The postmaster was amazed. He said, "How long has she been missing?"

The man said, "It has been seven days."

"You have come to report this after seven days?"

"I wanted to give her a chance. The farther away she can get the better," the man said. "Blessed is that man, his paradise is certain. He has turned me into a monk without any effort on my part."

No. Neither by renouncing wealth, nor the wife nor the husband, nor the marketplace, because... You should understand a small sutra of psychology very clearly. Whosoever you escape from, whosoever you wish to shut your eyes upon, you will find that person standing in front of your mind's eye – it is the weak person who escapes, it is the one gripped with fear who runs away, but you will not be free of the other by doing this.

And moreover, even if you do renounce the world and run away from your wife, what difference does it make? Inside you, the desire for the woman is present. It was there even when the wife was not there. It is because of it that you had sought out a wife in the first place. That desire will compel you to seek out a wife again. It does not make any difference what their faces look like. The faces can be different: some other woman, some other man.

You can renounce the palace and live in a hut, but that is not the real issue. The palace was "mine," now this hut will be "mine." You would have given your life for that palace; now you will give it for this hut. The real question is about "mine." About that there is no change.

So when I say that for an hour or a half hour sit down with closed eyes, what I am saying to you is that for an hour or for half an hour forget the other. There are twenty-four hours in a day. Give twenty-three hours to the whole world, to the marketplace, to your business, to your household – give it to anyone or to anything you want – but don't you even have that much right that you can save one hour just for yourself? Perhaps it may be very difficult to save all twenty-four hours; saving just one hour is possible. And then I am not saying to you that in order to save this one hour you have to go and sit in some cave in the Himalayas. Your house is sufficient, and the easiest place because you are familiar with all that is there, so to forget everything for an hour is less difficult.

If not today then tomorrow, if not tomorrow then the day after – soon that time comes when you can just simply sit. Images will come, do not take any interest in them – neither in favor nor against. Let them come and go. It is a pathway, a pathway of the mind and it is being walked upon. Just keep watching, sitting on the wayside. And you will be surprised, surprised by the greatest mystery of life: that if you go on watching as a witness – just witnessing, as if you have nothing to do with who is coming and who is going, you simply go on sitting quietly by the wayside – soon that time will come when the crowd of traffic will start to wane.

…Because there is a reason for this crowd being there on the pathway: you have invited it. Up until now, you have welcomed it; it is not there uninvited. And when it notices that you have become so indifferent that you don't even look back to see who has come and who has gone – whether it was a good person or a bad, beautiful or ugly, your own or a stranger – all this crowd will slowly start to disappear.

The process of meditation is very easy. Only a small capacity for patience is needed. And what have you got to lose? Even if you don't reach anywhere, at least you will have rested for an hour. But I know, from my own experience and from the experience of thousands whom I have helped pass through this process, that one day the hour comes – that great hour – when the pathway of the mind becomes empty. Not even dust arises; nothing remains to be known. And when there remains nothing to be known, only the knower remains. And that knower is not left with any option other than to know itself. To know is its nature. If you give some toy, a rattle, it goes into knowing that. But now, suddenly, there is nothing. Now, it can only know itself. And if someone has tasted himself even once, he has tasted deathlessness. Then there is neither darkness nor unconsciousness.

And then that one hour will slowly, slowly spread through all your twenty-four hours. You still remain in the marketplace, you still live in your house; your wife will be the same, your children will be the same, but you will not be the same. A revolution will have taken place in your life. All the perspectives of your seeing, your eyes will have been transformed. A peace…and a peace that passeth all understanding. And a light…a light that has neither oil nor wick – that exists without either and hence it never dies.

Without this experience the whole of life is a waste. And to attain to this experience is to attain to that ultimate opulence which never comes to an end. Then you can share it with both your hands, but you cannot exhaust it. It is this state of opulence, affluence, that we have called godliness in India. Our word *aishwarya* for opulence comes from the word *Ishwar* for godliness. Such a meaning given to godliness does not exist in any other language of the world.

Let me repeat it, so it remains in your memory.

The first thing: what you see as "understanding of the intellect" is not even that.

The second thing: what you are thinking to be very difficult is very easy, very natural. You have just never tried it.

Your entire education and teaching, your whole society, your conditionings, teach you to run after others. They teach you ambition for wealth, for position, for status, for fame. It is our misfortune that so far we haven't even been able to create a society that teaches you some of the secrets of how to know yourself. And there is no higher dignity than that, and there is no higher longing than that.

It is a very strange world. Here, people carrying an emperor within are moving around as beggars. The very people meant to be emperors are wandering around, carrying begging bowls in their hands. Just a little effort... But your society and your conditionings scare you. They say to you: "Knowing oneself? That takes lifetimes. That happens only once in a while, in the life of some incarnation of God, in the life of some *tirthankara*, in the life of some messiah, some prophet, some son of God. You are just a poor, ordinary man. You need not fall in this trap. You need not take up this trouble in your hand. It is beyond you."

I say to you, this is your birthright, and it does not require your becoming a *tirthankara*. Of course, when this phenomenon takes place in you, you become a *tirthankara*. It does not require being a messiah. Of course, when this phenomenon takes place in you, you become a messiah. To be a messiah is not the initial requirement. It is the final outcome.

I ask for just an hour from you – and you can't be that poor and helpless that you cannot give one hour out of twenty-four. Nobody is that poor. And I do not ask you to go to the temple or to go to the mosque, because as I see it, the temples, mosques, churches and *gurudwaras* have proved dangerous. They have created the idea that godliness is not in your house. I say to you that godliness is wherever you are, so wherever you sit is a holy place. Just sit a little silently, sit a little calmly, and if it takes a little more or a little less time, do not become impatient.

And people are so full of impatience. For an ordinary education that leaves them at the most a clerk in some office, they are ready to spend one third of their lives. And after wandering through universities and colleges for twenty-five years of their lives they will now wander through offices. And yet people do not consider that I am asking for only one hour – and that one hour's experience will take you to that point, to that experience of the immortal nectar, to the eternal, for the attainment of which, this very world is a school.

Osho.
You have mentioned two paths to godliness: love and
meditation. My situation is that love just doesn't arise in my
heart. Not that I don't want to love somebody, it just isn't
my type of personality. I like being quiet and sitting silently, so
I chose the path of meditation and started practicing witnessing.
Now the difficulty is that as I become aware and begin to watch
that I am watching the thoughts, the thoughts stop and a
momentary bliss arises – and then again the crowded traffic
of thoughts is there. And then again and again my watching
them, and again and again the same repetition.
There seems to be no progress in me. Am I making a mistake?
Or is my choice of the path of meditation wrong?
Please tell me my path so that more time is not wasted and
I don't miss you.

It is true that in order to attain to the ultimate truth, love and meditation are the two paths. But this does not mean that the meditator will be without love. Nor does it mean that the lover will not have to bother about meditation.

This appears a little bit complicated. Only initially is it a question of choosing. If you have chosen love to be your path, meditation will follow you like a shadow. Because if love doesn't bring meditation with it, it is not love, it is only lust. After all, what is the difference between love and lust? Only this much: that there is no shadow of meditation behind lust, and behind love there is the shadow of meditation.

And if you have chosen the path of meditation, that does not mean that you will become loveless, a blockhead. Meditation will be your spiritual discipline, but flowers of love will still start blooming in your life.

Love and meditation are only a matter of your leaning. Otherwise they are like two wings of a bird: if one is cut, the bird cannot fly. They are your two feet, they are like two oars for rowing a boat. If one oar is missing, the boat will start circling on the same spot.

This is where you have made the mistake. You did not understand the meaning of love. The meaning you took for love is only what can be understood in Mumbai: that one goes to Chowpatty Beach and flirts around, and understands the meaning of "love."

Love is goodwill toward the whole of existence; love is compassion unaddressed. Love is bliss – like when a flower blooms, its fragrance spreads all around. It does not seek particular nostrils.

I have heard…

There was a Buddhist nun in China. She was deeply in love with Buddha – at least that is what she thought.

She sold all her belongings and got a small statue of Buddha made of solid gold. She used to worship the statue every day, but there was one difficulty. When she would burn incense, the smoke could not be relied upon. Sometimes it would go toward her Buddha statue and at other times it would go somewhere else. The smoke was not concerned, it would go wherever the winds took it, so the nun became very disturbed.

Her troubles only increased because the great temple she was staying in…. Perhaps it is the greatest surviving temple in the whole world. It would have taken centuries to build it. It was carved out of an entire mountain and there are one thousand statues of Buddha in it. It is called "The Temple of the One Thousand Buddhas," and every statue is more beautiful than the next. So the nun's problem was that when she would burn incense for her Buddha, or offer flowers, the other rogue Buddhas would enjoy the fragrance too. This was intolerable – and this she thought to be love!

She brooded over what to do. And then she made a funnel from a hollow bamboo. After burning incense she would guide the smoke through the bamboo to the nostrils of her own Buddha statue.

Now the poor Buddha, the golden Buddha, cannot say anything to the nun: "What is all this nonsense you are up to, you naive woman?" Buddha's nose, his eyes, his whole face, became black. Then she became very nervous.

She went to the priest of the temple and said, "I am in trouble. What shall I do? If I do not use the bamboo funnel then the fragrance of the incense does not reach to my Buddha. And there is such a crowd of all these rogue Buddhas – one thousand of them are present, all around. I cannot guess which one will start pulling the fragrant smoke toward himself. So I made this funnel, which has now created new trouble. The face of my Buddha has become black."

The priest answered, "What you have done is what is happening in the whole world. Every lover blackens the face of the beloved."

And people call this love. "May my fragrance, my love, not reach someone else" – and so we all build bamboo funnels in our own way. A Hindu will marry a Hindu; a Mohammedan will marry a Mohammedan. And after the marriage things are also not secure. It is a big world: thousands of Buddhas, all sorts of rogues, are wandering around, so he will keep all the doors and windows closed – even if the loved one suffocates and along with that, he himself suffocates. And this suffocation is happening in every house. I have been a guest in thousands of houses, and I have seen people suffocating in every house. The wife is weeping because she married the man she loved.

It is very surprising. It seems as if people should instead love their enemies, or at least the marriages should be made between enemies. You can love anyone, but marry only the enemy, the arch enemy, because the way you are going to behave later on....

Your idea of love is wrong, and if as a woman you feel that there is no love inside you, this is impossible. Just as there is water beneath the earth everywhere – it is a different matter that somewhere it is below fifty feet, somewhere below sixty – similarly there is love inside every person. Man is somewhat hard, the well has to be dug deeper. The woman is more fluid and not that hard. She requires less digging before the water is found. But sometimes it also occurs that what we see happening all around us in the name of love makes us hard, makes us afraid, scared: "If this is love, then may the Lord save me from it."

You may have similarly created a wall around yourself. Demolish it. It is not necessary that in order to demolish that wall you will have to marry and have children. Only this much will do: that between you and the greater human society, between you and the flora and fauna, there remains no wall. We are all connected. We are all together. No matter how far away we may be, yet we are always very close. After all, we all belong to the same existence. We are all born out of it and one day we will all disappear into it.

So, my first suggestion will be to drop this false idea that you have no love in you, and love is not your path. Without love you will become dry, without love you will be like a thirsty person in the desert. Demolish this wall.

I am not saying for you to walk the path of love. I am only saying to remove the idea that you have about love. Walk the path of meditation: you like it, you find it interesting. The moment you let go of your wrong notion about love, you will find that your notion of meditation – your path of meditation – has become easy on its own, has become juicy on its own. The difficulties that were felt until yesterday are, of their own accord, no longer felt.

You have asked: "I sit down. I watch the thoughts as a witness. Sometimes the thoughts stop and for a moment great bliss is felt. And then the thoughts begin again, and so it goes on. How long will this continue?"

This will continue until you rectify the first mistake. That experience of bliss that you feel for a moment is unable to grow and become bigger because you have obstructed the love. If this small moment of bliss is attained and the dam of love also bursts, then the whole stream can start flowing within you as well. Then, bigger and bigger gaps of silence will start appearing; for longer and longer intervals there will be no trace of thoughts. And a new experience will take place: that here the meditation is growing and there, behind it, the fragrance of love is spreading. The day that meditation and love do not appear as two, know that the destination has been reached.

The day meditation is love and love is meditation, know that the temple has been reached. Now there is nowhere else to go. It is here where one is meant to arrive.

So one chooses in the beginning, but in the end there is no choosing. In the end, love and meditation both become one. Meditation makes you meet yourself and love makes you meet the whole.

If you stop just after meeting yourself, this whole existence will remain separate from you. That attainment will be incomplete. And if you meet all, but not yourself, what kind of meeting will that be? The day you meet yourself, if you also meet the whole, then the attainment is complete.

Let me repeat it so that you don't forget it: Your notion of love is wrong, drop it.

Love does not mean lust or desire. Love means goodwill for all.

It is said of Gautam Buddha that he would say to each of his *bhikshu*, "When you meditate, when you become full of bliss, do not forget to do one thing. And that is, share your bliss with the whole universe. Only after that, get up from the meditation. May it not happen that meditation also becomes a miserliness. May it not happen that you also start depositing meditation in your safe. Whatever you attain to, share it. Then tomorrow more will come; share that also. And the more you share, the more will come to you yourself."

One man stood up and he said, "Alright. Your wish is our law. I want just one exception to be made."

Buddha said, "What exception?"

The man said, "I meditate and I will continue to do so, and in accordance with your wish, I will pray to the universe to partake of the experience. But I want just a small exception to be made, and that is: I want to exclude my neighbor from this, because I cannot bear the idea of that wretched fellow benefiting from my meditation. Just this much I ask from you – just a neighbor. I am ready to share meditation with the whole world, with anybody living on the farthest star – I wouldn't mind that – but with this good-for-nothing...?"

Buddha said, "Then it is very difficult. You didn't get the point at all! The question is not that one is to share with this one or that one. The question is not that one is to share with one's own people and not with others. The question is not that one will give a little extra to the friend and a little less to the enemy. The question is that one will give, unconditionally, and will not ask who the receiver is. And that's where you have got stuck. Your meditation will not move forward. The moon and stars don't have any meaning for you, so you are ready to share your love with them, your meditation, your bliss with them. But the neighbor?"

So Buddha said, "Now, I say this to you. Forget all about the others, about the moon, about the stars. Only make this prayer every day after the meditation: 'May all the bliss from my meditation reach to my neighbor.' In your case, only this much is enough. For others, even the whole world is small; for you, even your neighbor seems to be far bigger than the whole world."

The meaning of love is only this much: "May my bliss, the happiness of my life, the fragrance of my life, reach to all unconditionally, without any reason."

So the first thing you need to remember is that your old concept of love is wrong. And the second thing: that moment of bliss which comes to you in your meditation, don't abandon it in panic, because it is that moment....

It is like how tiny the Ganges is at the Gangotri – the place of its origin. It is so tiny that the Hindus have created a mouth of a cow there called Gomukh and the Ganges emerges out of that cow mouth. And that same Ganges, after making a journey of thousands of miles, becomes so vast that where it meets the ocean its name has become Gangasagar, "the oceanic Ganges." It is difficult to see its other shore.

That tiny moment that you glimpse is a Gangotri as yet. If you reorient your love, it will not be long before it becomes a Gangasagar.

Its becoming a Gangasagar is certain. The laws of existence do not change; they are the same forever. If ever something goes amiss, it is because of us. There is no bias in the laws of the universe.

Osho,
All the mystics have called the heart the door to spiritual
experience and the mind the door to thinking and the intellect.
What is the difference between the heart and the mind? What
is the difference between the heart and the soul? How to
make this difference distinct and how to recognize it?

Thinking is the very first door available to man. Man first of all learns how to think. The capability of man to think and to reflect is called intellect, and it is this intellect that all our educational institutions make skillful. And that is why thinking is plentiful in the world, but not love. And it doesn't take long for a world in which thinking is plentiful but not love to turn into a hell, because thinking has nothing to do with what is right and what is wrong. Thinking is a prostitute.

In Greece, there was a big philosophical tradition before Socrates. The name of the people in that tradition was the Sophists. Their work was to teach thinking to aristocrats, princes or whosoever was ready to pay their fee. They were available to teach the process of thinking, the process of logic. They did not subscribe to any particular principle of their own. They just taught the process of thinking and the process of logic, then it was up to you what you used it for – for good or for bad. In the same way that a sword can cut someone's throat or can also save someone's throat from being cut; in the same way that poison can kill a person, or in an expert's hands, can also save someone's life, so the whole work of the Sophists was: "We will teach you this art of swordsmanship and then for what you use the sword, for what you aim to use it, all that is your business. We have got nothing to do with all that."

Xeno, a very thoughtful young man, enlisted himself in a great Sophist's school for training. The rule of the Sophists was that one had to deposit half the fee at the time of enrollment and the remaining half would be paid after the training, whenever the person won his first debate. They were so sure of their science, they knew the person would certainly win.

Xeno deposited half his fee and completed his training. Many moons came and passed, many months came and passed, and the teacher was after him for the remaining half of his fee. But Xeno said, "Let the condition be fulfilled: when I win some debate I will pay the fee. But I have decided that I will not go for any debate; even if somebody announces the day as night, I will not argue. I will say, yes, it is nighttime. In order to avoid a debate, I am not going to make any fuss over anything. And until I win a debate I am not going to pay the remaining fee. And you know me well, after all I am your disciple and I have learnt the art from you!

The master thought, "This is too much! This man has turned out to be quite outrageous. Something will have to be done." A teacher, after all, will have to prove his superiority. So he made a case against Xeno in the court, claiming that Xeno had not paid him the second half of his fee: in accordance with the tradition of his lineage of thinking, now the second half had to be recovered. If Xeno were to win the case, the master would ask the court to help him recover the amount due, since Xeno was the winner. But if Xeno were to lose, the master would catch him by the neck outside the court and ask for the fee due, citing the judgment of the law court that had been given in his favor.

But Xeno was, after all, his disciple; their ways of thinking were similar. The logic, the sword of the two was the same. He thought, "Good. If I lose in the court, I will ask the court to instruct my teacher never again to ask me for the remaining fee since I have lost my very first debate. But if I win in the court, which is very probable because all the arguments are in my favor, then I will say: 'So far I haven't gone for a debate – so what fee?' And this certainly was the condition for payment. And if I win in the court, I will catch my teacher outside the court and say, 'Good afternoon! I cannot go against the ruling of the court. I abide by the laws.'"

Thoughts are prostitutes. Thoughts in themselves have no life-philosophy of their own. Thoughts in themselves have no sight of their own. But we educate people to gain skill in that very blindness. Hidden deeper below thought is our heart, but so far all societies have been trying to prevent man from feeling his heart because the heart is dangerous. The heart does not know logic, it knows love. Thought can be used – you can be turned into a soldier, you can be turned into a clerk – but what use will you make of love? Society has no use for love, on the contrary, society is in danger from love, because today you love someone, tomorrow you may start loving someone else, the day after tomorrow still someone else. So how can the society go on organizing things in the midst of all this?

In order to destroy love, society invented marriage and made a thousand and one rules that declared true love to be that which never changes – in spite of the fact that whatsoever is real in this world goes on changing every day, and it is only the false things that never change. Plastic flowers do not change; a rose's real flowers go on changing daily.

There are many dangers with love. It is very difficult to make any-body a soldier. In order to make someone a soldier, it is necessary that his love is utterly butchered, otherwise whenever he takes a gun in his hand to kill the enemy, his heart will say to him, "This man must have a mother, just as you have; this man must have a wife, just as you have. In the same way my wife was weeping uncontrollably as she was saying goodbye to me, similarly his wife must also have wept. And this man must have small children whom I am about to make into orphans. And he must have an old father for whom he may be the only supporting link. What is this that I am about to do, and why? This man has done nothing wrong to me. I have simply taken up a job for a wretched one hundred rupee salary – and I am ready to take his life? And this poor fellow – also for a wretched hundred rupee job – is holding a gun to my chest."

If there is even a small ray of love in them, they will drop their guns and embrace each other, because both will be facing the same problem. And those on whom these guns ought to be aimed are sitting in the capitals.

You will be amazed to know that in the Second World War, the American soldiers who were middle-aged or older behaved in the way a soldier is expected to behave: they ran a wholesale business in killing. But thirty percent of the younger soldiers did not kill a single person. In the morning they would go to the front with their guns and by the evening they would return with their guns, without having killed anybody.

When this became the subject of a psychological study, it created a fear across the whole of America. If this news were to spread through the entire younger generation like a wildfire – and thirty percent is no small number – and the American youth were to ask why they should kill someone who has done no wrong to them, then the American pride that they are the greatest superpower in the world would simply go down the drain. But the people to whom this pride belongs are in Washington D.C., and the people who must kill and be killed have no name or address.

No society wants to allow your heart and your love to develop. It stops it in every possible way. And the biggest difficulty is that your mind is the most superficial level. Deeper than that is your heart, and even deeper than that is your being. Because your heart is not allowed to develop, all possibilities of reaching the being cease, all doors close. Hence if today there is such a shortage of people who know their souls, it is not surprising. It should not have been like this, because people have been on the search for the soul for thousands of years. The number of self-realized ones should have increased, but their numbers have gone down day by day.

All the powers of the world – who are against love and self-realization – will become the enemy of any person talking of how the doors of your heart can be opened and how the flower of your being can bloom.

I have harmed no one in any way, but America has managed to get all the non-communist countries of the world to agree that I should not be allowed a place even to put my feet down. And the communist countries already felt disturbed by me.

Such a vast earth, and it has become so small for me! What is their fear?

Their fear is very fundamental. Their fear is that I am giving the message of love to their youth. Their fear is that I am sharing inspiration for meditation amongst their youth. Their fear is that today, for the first time, tens of millions of people around the earth have agreed to enter a process of meditation and to dive into the wondrous ocean of love, without being bothered if they are Hindus or Mohammedans or Christians or Zoroastrians or Jews. This is their fear.

Without any crime, today I am enemy number one in the eyes of America. In their own courts they couldn't prove any crime against me – because how can they? No law in the world says that love is a sin, no law in the world says that to know the soul is a crime. So what are they to prove? No law in the world says that meditation and enlightenment lead one to hell. So what are they to prove in their courts?

Just four days ago the Attorney General of America, answering journalists in a press gathering said… Someone had asked why I was not punished, why I was not sentenced to jail. The logic of his answer is worth paying attention to. He said, "We were interested in destroying the commune Osho had established. That was our priority, that was our foremost task."

And what was that commune? It was a small gathering of five thousand people who were meditating in a desert where no American had any business to come, nor was invited. The nearest American town from us was twenty miles away – a small village – and a slightly bigger town was thirty miles away. What trouble could we have been to them?

One thing had become very clear to them: that if the commune was to be destroyed, it was necessary that I should be sent out of the country first – because those five thousand sannyasins had declared that if an attempt was made to arrest me, that could occur only after dealing with all of them. That is why their desire to arrest me had

107

lingered on for two years. Every day, there would be news that "today an arrest warrant will certainly arrive" and near the commune, in the village twenty miles away, they had stationed the army, so that if it became necessary they would massacre five thousand people.

And these five thousand sannyasins had done no harm to them. Their only crime was that they had turned a desert into an oasis and had given America a glimpse of the eternal sweetness of meditation for the first time. And for the first time a place was created in America that existed nowhere else in that country – a *tirtha*, a sacred place of pilgrimage. Thousands of sannyasins were coming to the commune from all over the world every year. America should have been happy that we were giving their land a sacredness, we were giving a gift of religiousness to their irreligious society. But perhaps therein lay their fear.

Think from the intellect, but remember to think in a way that takes you toward the heart, not away from it. Only then are you an intelligent person. Love, but love in a way that does not take you through the dark valleys of lust rather than leading you toward your being. And meditate in order that one day you are able to light that lamp within you which will never die. He who lights that lamp experiences the fulfillment of his life. And he who dies without lighting that lamp, lived in vain, dies in vain.

To conclude, I want to repeat that to experience this fulfillment is your birthright.

CHAPTER 8

THE CALL OF YOUR OWN
INTERIORITY

Osho,
I feel very worried seeing your state of health. You have been
pouring out your soul as you reach out to the world, but instead
of changing, people wanted to destroy you. Why do you still
make such an effort?

The body is bound to be destroyed. If it is destroyed on the path of love, there is no greater blessing. The body is bound to become tired and tattered, but if through it, I am able to give birth to rays of bliss in some people's lives, it is a blessing. It makes no difference whether, upon hearing me, people change or not. Along with the experience of truth, comes compassion as its shadow saying, "Whether someone is going to change or not, at least give the call. Let no blame rest with you – that you did not give the call. Let no one be able to say that you remained silent."

I no longer need the body. My journey has come to a completion – and since a long time. I have known what there is to be known, I have attained what there is to be attained: now there is nothing beyond that. During the days that are left before this body takes leave on its own accord, if in the lives of even a few people some lamps can be lit, if in the lives of even a few people some smile can spread... And in a certain number of people's lives the lamps have begun to light up, the smile has begun to spread, and the dancing bells on some people's feet, and the flute at some people's lips... Those who want to destroy me are unnecessarily feeling disturbed. I will leave by myself – who lives forever?

But the efforts of those who want to destroy me are perhaps part of the laws of nature and destiny. As an effort to destroy me grows, with that same intensity the inner beings of some people will awaken. If I create ten enemies, one friend will also be born. And I count friends – what is the need to be bothered with enemies?

And I have made enough friends in this world. Perhaps it has never happened before – because Buddha's ceaseless effort was confined to the state of Bihar, Jesus' to Judea. Socrates never even ventured out of the city of Athens. But I have given the call to the whole world. Thousands of people have heard that call. Tens of millions of enemies have been created, but I keep no count of enemies; I am keeping a count of my friends. And as the number of enemies has grown, in that same proportion the strength of friends, the courage of friends has also grown. Their determination to transform has strengthened. And seeing that so many people are willing to destroy me, many people have become willing to be destroyed for me. So there is no need to worry.

Not for one single moment has the idea ever crossed my mind that I might have taken a wrong step. In any case, this body ultimately falls away – and mostly it falls away when you are in your bed. Ninety-nine percent of people die in their beds. That is why I say to you: "Don't sleep in the bed." There is nothing in this world as dangerous as a bed – ninety-nine percent of people die there! In the middle of the night, silently get out and sleep on the floor. You may start in your bed so no one says anything, but later in the night, very silently get out, if you want to survive. Remember how many people have died in bed! It is very rare that someone dies on the cross – the numbers are negligible – but you have a great love for your bed, and a great animosity toward the cross!

The body will certainly go. It is meant to go. Whosoever has come here has only come in order to go. And because this body of mine is not going to come back again, and the one who is speaking through this breath is never going to speak through any breath again... Its resting point has come, its final destination has arrived: it is my last life and my last journey. In these final days, if I can bring the message to as many people as possible... No matter what tortures I may have to go through, nothing can be taken away from me. If someone takes away that which death will take away in any case, it has not been taken away from me. It has been taken away from death, I have nothing to do with it.

I am happy because I have been able to speak my heart to so many people. No one has ever been able to do this before in the world. And the number of people who love me – no one has ever been loved so much in his lifetime. And the number of people who hate me – No one has ever been hated so much in his lifetime either. This, too, I consider to be a blessing – because it is possible that those who hate me today may love me tomorrow. It is not very difficult for hate to transform into love. Perhaps hate is their way of arriving at the temple of love.

I remember a small incident.

There have been Hasidic mystics amongst the Jews.

The mystic who gave birth to the Hasidic tradition, Baalshem, wrote his first book. He sent his disciple with a copy of it as a gift to the highest rabbi, the highest religious head of the Jews. He told the disciple, "Take this book, give it personally into the hands of the chief rabbi, not to anybody else. And the reason I am sending you is so that you can watch the reaction of the rabbi very carefully: whatever he says, whatever emotions show on his face, take good note of it all. You must report every detail to me without making a mistake. And because you are my most alert disciple, I am sending you."

Hasidism is a revolutionary tradition. The Jewish rabbi is an old and rotten thing of dead rites and rituals. In order to be a Hasid one has to pass through a revolution; in order to be a Jew it is enough to be born into a Jewish family.

So when the disciple arrived there, the chief rabbi and his wife were both having tea, sitting in their garden. He put Baalshem's book into the hands of the rabbi. The rabbi took it and asked, "Whose book is it?"

And as the disciple said, "This is Baalshem's first book, the first compilation of his words," a fire came into the eyes of the rabbi, as if the face of a demon overtook his face. He threw the book away, onto the road outside his garden, and said, "How dare you enter this house? And how could you put that filthy book into my hands? Now I will have to take a shower."

The disciple watched all this.

And the rabbi's wife said, "Don't be so angry. You have such a vast library. There is no harm if this book also remains lying there in some corner. And even if you had to throw the book away, you could have done so after the young man had gone."

The disciple went back to Baalshem. Baalshem asked him, "What happened?"

The disciple said, "There is no possibility of the rabbi ever having a change of heart, but perhaps his wife may someday change." And then he reported the whole story.

Baalshem started laughing. He said, "You are naive. You have no idea about human psychology. And if you don't believe me, go back and see. The rabbi must have picked up the book by now and be reading it. And there is no chance of his wife being transformed. That woman doesn't even have hate in her heart; love is a far away call. But the rabbi became excited, emotionally charged. My work is done. Just go back – the rabbi will be reading the book."

The disciple went back and he was astonished at what he saw: the book had disappeared from the road. He peeped in. The rabbi was in the garden and was browsing through the book, and the rabbi's wife was not there.

Hate is the inverted form of love. It is love doing a headstand. So the number of the people who love me is quite big, but the number of people who hate me is even bigger, and I am grateful to both, because with those who love me, there is no question that they will not dive into my love. But those who hate me – if not today then tomorrow, if not tomorrow then the day after – they will pick up that book from the road and read it. There is no way they can avoid me. By hating me, they have created a relationship with me. Although they have created it in anger, a relationship is relationship.

I can understand the state of your mind. I can understand your love. But I want to assure you that I am living only because of your love, otherwise for me there is simply no reason for living. When I see the light shining in your eyes, I think to myself, "A little bit longer, perhaps a few more will enter the tavern, perhaps a few more will be filled with remembrance to drink this wine."

Don't worry about my body. That is for existence to worry about. Only worry about one thing: that as long as I am here, make this gathering of drunkards grow as large as you can. Because if this gathering keeps on growing and growing, then I assure you that I will stay amongst you.

Osho,
Have you stopped initiating people into sannyas and creating
disciples? Am I to be deprived of becoming your disciple?

A disciple is not made, one has to become one. When you love someone, do you first ask the person? Do you first take the permission of the person? Love just happens. Love neither obeys any order nor takes any permission, nor does it believe in any modes or methods.

What is discipleship?

It is the highest, the deepest name of love. If you want to love me, how can I stop you? If you shed tears in love for me, how can I stop you? And if you dive into what I call meditation, how can I stop you? Whosoever wants to be a disciple, no one can stop him. And that is why I have dropped all the formalities that were there for making someone a disciple, because now I want only those who are coming toward me of their own accord, not via some other route. Now, the whole responsibility is yours.

For instance, we teach students in the first grade: a is for apple, g is for Ganesh. In fact, previously g used to be for Ganesh, now it is for *gadha*, the donkey. It is a secular state. Here it is not appropriate that the word Ganesh appears in a textbook. But neither does Ganesh have anything to do with g or gadha. It is just a way to teach a small child. The child finds gadha or Ganesh more interesting. He doesn't find any interest in the letter g. But slowly, slowly gadha will be forgotten, Ganesh will be forgotten, only g will remain, and only g will be used.

If you keep having to read a for apple, g for Ganesh, by the time you enter the university, there will be no opportunity to study. Even to read one complete sentence will be impossible. And after reading it, it will become difficult to understand what the meaning is, because who knows how many donkeys and Ganeshas and mangoes will be in the sentence?

There are pictures in small children's textbooks – colored pictures, big pictures, and a few letters. And with every move to a higher class the pictures go on becoming smaller and the letters become more and more. Slowly, the pictures disappear altogether and only the letters remain. In university classes, there are no pictures, only letters, the *akshar*.

Our word *akshar* is also very lovely. It means that which will never be destroyed. So, Ganesha can be destroyed, *gadhas* can be destroyed, but the *akshar* will always remain. It never ceases.

So when I started, I had to initiate people into sannyas, to make people disciples. But how long can one play the joke of *gadhas* and Ganeshas; apples and pineapples? Now, sannyas has matured. Now, formalities no longer have an important place.

Now, if you are in love, become a disciple. It is not something even to be talked about. Now, no need even to let anyone know: if it is your feeling, be a sannyasin. Now, the whole responsibility is yours. This is the sign of being mature. How long can I walk along with you, holding your hand? Before my hands are removed, I have to let go of your hands by myself, so that you can stand on your own feet – relying on your own hands, your own responsibility – and walk.

No, there is no need for you to stop from becoming a disciple. Nor can anyone prevent you from becoming a sannyasin. But now it is your decision alone, according to the thirst and the call of your own interiority.

I am with you, my blessings are with you, but now I will not explain to you about becoming a sannyasin or ask you to meditate. Now, I will only explain this much: what meditation is. If only this much can trigger a thirst in you, then meditate. Now, I will not tell you to love. Now, I will only describe love and everything else to you. If no song arises in your heart – even upon hearing the unique and mysterious description of love – then nothing will come out of commanding it from you either. And if a song arises, then it is not a matter of giving and taking: you can be a disciple, you can meditate, you can become a sannyasin, you can attain to enlightenment, you can achieve the ultimate treasure of this life that we have called *moksha*, the ultimate liberation.

But now you have to do all this. Gone are the days of someone giving you a push from behind. Now, you are completely free. Your own wish, your own joy, your own ecstasy are the deciding factors.

CHAPTER 9

FREEDOM
FROM THE PAST

Osho,
These days in our country, the policy makers are talking again
and again of "taking the country into the twenty-first century."
Particularly in the last one and a half to two years
this discussion has escalated.
Do you think this is possible in the present situation?

The very first thing is whether or not this country is even in the twentieth century! India must be taken into the twenty-first century – that is understandable – but who will take you? Here, people are still living thousands of years in the past. The leaders of this country, even people like Mahatma Gandhi, think that all the discoveries and inventions that have taken place after the invention of the spinning wheel should be destroyed, that the spinning wheel is the ultimate science. Mahatma Gandhi was against railway trains, against telephones, against the telegraph. If he is listened to...

And the leaders of this country have been following his ideas, at least they have been pretending to, at least they have been keeping the "Gandhi cap" on, at least they have been wearing khadi – clothes made from handspun yarn.

If he is listened to then this country will fall back at least two thousand years. Forget about the twenty-first century, even if it reaches the first century one should be thankful.

The minds of the people who are talking about taking India into the twenty-first century are filled with such rotten ideas, ideas that have already been discarded all over the world but which are still alive in India.

The idea is very pleasant, that "Let us move into the twenty-first century, and also *before* others," but we are still sitting in bullock carts, while others have reached to the moon. Yes, once in a while in stories we also arrive at the moon, but even if we reach the moon, we will still be what we are.

I have heard...

When an American landed on the moon for the first time he was puzzled to see that a Hindu monk was sitting there in meditation by a fire. He said, "This is too much! We have almost killed ourselves working so hard to get here. We have spent billions of dollars on the project, and this junkie is already sitting here by his fire in meditation. It must be some spiritual miracle."

So the American went over and touched the monk's feet in reverence, upon which the monk opened his eyes and asked him, "Have you got a cigarette on you? It has been such a long time since I enjoyed an American cigarette."

The American man said, "Here, take the cigarette, but tell me, how did you reach here?"

The monk said, "What is so difficult about it? Are you aware of the population of our country? It was four hundred million when the country became independent, now it is nine hundred million, and by the end of this century it will cross the one billion mark. We have been listening to all your pomp and show – that you are developing this, you are organizing that, and we thought, 'Why indulge in such meaning-less ideas? Let's just stand one on top of the other, like the multistory houses in Mumbai.' And because I am a monk I stood on top of them all. Now all those fools have left me here and have gone back to their jobs and businesses."

It is easy to enter the twenty-first century in stories, and whether you talk to the naive masses for whom ten is the limit, who can't even count up to twenty-one, of the twenty-first century or the thirty-first century, makes no difference at all. They think that when you say something, it must be right.

And no one believes in any of the leaders' statements any more, because in these forty years they have only deceived people. For forty years the Indian leaders have been handing out deception after deception. Forty years ago there was a feeling of respect in the minds of the public toward these people, toward their fathers and grand-fathers. Today even in the minds of the illiterate people of India there is no respect toward the politicians, only insult. The politicians are not counted amongst anyone other than the thieves and hooligans – and they should not be. Thieves and the hooligans just snatch or steal something small from people here and there, like pickpocketing. And these politicians are destroying the very potential of the whole country. They are destroying the very future of the country.

But they have to use big words. Except for their words they have nothing else. "Twenty-first century"! But look at the condition of the people of India in general. The meaning of ushering in the twenty-first century will be that all the values of life will change.

Right now people's behavior toward the *harijans*, the untouch-ables, is the same as was meted out to them five thousand years ago. And the habit of lying has entered so deeply into our psyche...what to say of the ordinary people? I am not talking about the ordinary people. Mahatma Gandhi himself made the frequent statement that India's first president would be a woman and an untouchable. Now, as far as I understand it, neither was Dr Rajendra Prasad – the first president of India – a woman nor was he an untouchable, and it was Gandhi who chose him. What happened to all those old promises? Where did all that lofty talk disappear to? What of all those sweet intoxicating words you fed the harijans?

All that was simply politics because there was fear. The harijans wanted to separate under the leadership of Ambedkar. If the Mohammedans were asking for a separate country for themselves and their demand was being considered legitimate, and the Hindus wanted their own country, then the harijans who were one fourth of the Hindus and had been the exploited and the oppressed of this country for thousands of years... There is no people more oppressed than them in the world. But if they also wanted to have a separate country of their own, then Gandhi would go on *amaran anashan* – a fast unto death.

Amaran anashan? Amaran anashan has not happened even once, because orange juice is offered before the person's death comes close – that is always arranged beforehand. And the doctors were continuously making check-ups, and there was a commotion all over the country lest Mahatma Gandhi really died.

This changed the very focus; the actual issue of the harijans just evaporated. Ambedkar's own life fell under threat. People started pressurizing him to ask for forgiveness from Mahatma Gandhi and to say to him, "We are not going to demand a separate country or a separation of any kind." And Ambedkar's demand was legitimate, but who cares about legitimate and illegitimate when this is happening? Ambedkar also felt that if Gandhi died "My being killed will be no big deal, but the harijans will be burnt to ashes from one corner of this country to the other. Their huts will be burnt, their women will be raped, Gandhi's death will be revenged." The very issue of whether what he was saying was right or wrong, was put aside. The very focus had shifted.

The issue became whether or not it would be right to put the harijans into such a catastrophic position. Already the poor fellows had been in enough trouble – now this would be one more tragedy. So Ambedkar presented himself in front of Gandhi with a glass of orange juice, and asked for his forgiveness, knowing full well that this man was deceiving the harijans, this man was deceiving the country.

Harijans neither won the right to separation nor the right of a separate ballot. They had such a small demand: "Either give us a separate country or a right to a separate ballot," so that their voice could also reach the parliament and explain what they were enduring – which doesn't get reported in any news, even the news of it doesn't reach you.

And Gandhi had assured them, "Don't worry. Our first president will be a harijan, and not only a harijan but a woman, because women have been tortured much and the harijans have also been tortured much. All this will not be allowed to continue after our independence has come."

Freedom came – but neither did any harijan become the president

121

nor any woman. Freedom came and millions died, were robbed. Who knows how many children lost their lives, how many women were raped? Who knows how many people were burnt alive? Amazing freedom!

The whole business of partition could have been managed with love. But Mahatma Gandhi and his disciples did not let that happen and brought the situation to such a point that enmity reached its climax. So when partition took place violence was inevitable. This is what is happening in the Punjab, this is what is happening in Assam, this is what is happening in Kashmir. This will happen in every part of the country, and these dwarf politicians are trying to take the country into the twenty-first century!

You can only accomplish this in one way: get the calendar for the twenty-first century printed, hang it in your homes, and you will have reached the twenty-first century. Start using the dates of the twenty-first century. No one has any right to prevent us from this: "The calendar is ours. We are printing it. We don't want to live in the twentieth century, we want to live in the twenty-first century."

On the calendar you can reach, but not in real life. And you are not even ready to even hear those who are able take you there in real life.

I can take you into the twenty-first century, but you are not ready to hear me because arriving in the twenty-first century depends on two things.

First, you will have to be free of your past, you will have to become light. You are so badly tied to the past that you take one step forward and then take two steps back. You are tied to the past with everything. You will have to drop every relationship with the past. Just think: nature itself has not given you eyes in the back of your skull. Eyes are for looking ahead. What has passed has passed; what has gone has gone; what has withered has withered. Focus your eyes forward. But no! You are busy watching *Ramaleela,* the re-enactment of Rama's life.

There can be no *Ramaleela* in the twenty-first century. There is no place for Rama in the twenty-first century, because Rama's whole behavior is inhuman. He ordered molten lead to be poured into the ears of a young *sudra*, an untouchable, because he had heard some hymns of the Rig Veda. And it is the kingdom of this Rama that Mahatma Gandhi wants to bring back to this country – this cruelty, this inhumanness! And Rama still remains an incarnation of God. He is still your revered figure. Say goodbye to him now!

Just turn back and look: who are the people that you are entangled with, and what kind of people are they?

Krishna had sixteen thousand women out of whom only one, Rukmini, was his real wife. The poor woman doesn't even get much of a mention. Who bothers about his real wife? Who cares about one's own wife? Except for this one wife, all the other sixteen thousand were taken away from others. They were others' wives: they had children, husbands, old in-laws. Their families must have been ruined. Their only fault was that they were beautiful.

Once Krishna saw a woman and her beauty was noticed by him, he would not give a damn what effect it would have on others. The woman was simply carried away. His soldiers would forcibly take the woman away to Krishna's harem. And yet not a single man in India had the guts to raise a finger against Krishna: "Is this the man we call a total incarnation of God? If these are the qualities of a total incarnation of God then we don't want God reincarnating here. Now he should go somewhere else: there are so many stars and planets and constellations. Let him die wherever he pleases, but no more visits here."

I was taking a meditation camp in Gujarat. It was a beautiful, small place, Tulsi Shyam. Tulsi was one such wife who Krishna had abducted. In the temple is Krishna's statue with this abducted wife Tulsi. It should be in a prison, but unfortunately it is in the temple. The temple is in the valley and in the temple is this beautiful statue of Tulsi and Krishna. Above the valley, hidden at a distance in a cluster of bushes, is another small temple in which there is Rukmini's statue. The poor help-less woman is sitting there watching from her hideout what games her husband is playing.

You will have to change many of your values. It will be painful because there has been a great attachment to those values. You have never looked at their dark sides. No one has ever criticized them in front of you. We have forgotten to take a critical view. We just subscribe to blind faith, blind worship, blind belief. If you want to enter the twenty-first century, you will have to drop this blindness. Machines cannot take you there. Eyes, clear eyes, are needed so that they can see into the far distance.

And the eyes of a believer are such that they cannot even see what is nearby, what to say of seeing into the far distance?

You will have to learn to doubt, because it is the sword of doubt that will destroy your blind beliefs and superstitions and provide you with the opportunity for reflection, contemplation and meditation.

The science of the West has only been born over the past three hundred years. And it has been born fighting for every inch of its ground with Christianity, because Christianity has posed obstacles over even the smallest matters. The Bible says that the earth is flat; the findings of science say it is round. The Bible says that the sun goes around the earth, and science has found that the reality is just the opposite. It is the earth that goes around the sun.

When for the first time Galileo wrote in his book that the earth goes around the sun, this old man, who was almost on his deathbed, was dragged to the pope's court. And the pope told him, "Make amendments in your book otherwise you will be burned alive."

Galileo said, "I have no objection. I will change it in my book. I am not keen to be burned alive – after death one is burned anyway, but what is the hurry to be burned? As far as the book is concerned, I will make the changes. But I must say one thing: that making changes in my book will make no difference. The earth will still go on revolving around the sun. No matter how much I write something in my book, neither the sun nor the earth will read my book. And why are you so troubled? If a small line goes against the Bible, why does it disturb you so much?"

And what the pope said is worth keeping in mind. The pope said, "The disturbance is that if even one word of the Bible is proved wrong, doubts will start arising in people's minds that, who knows, if one thing has been found to be wrong, who knows what other things may also be wrong? Up until now they have been believing the Bible to be the word of God. But if God can also make mistakes, then how can the pope claim to be infallible? We will not tolerate anything that goes against what is written in the Bible."

But the struggle continued. For three hundred years science has fought for every inch of its ground.

There has been no such fight in this country. Here, in this country, you have only read science in the schools and the colleges. It has remained superficial. Someone is studying science and at the same time he is wearing an amulet of the monkey god tied onto his arm. Will these useless people take you into the twenty-first century? They go to sit for a science examination and first they go to the temple of the monkey god to offer a coconut for his blessings. The scientific approach has not yet entered our psyche. All our science is secondhand. We study it and get trained in it, but inside we remain the same. Inside the basis of all our belief systems remains unchanged.

One of my friends was a well-known doctor. Who knows how many endless numbers of patients he had cured, and his fame ran far and wide. But when his wife became ill one day, he said to me, "I have tried every treatment but nothing is helping her. My servant tells me that if some religious saint gives her his blessings then something may be possible."

I said, "You are such a great doctor. You know that when there is sickness there is some cause behind it. Diagnose it and try to eradicate the cause. Your wife did not fall ill because of some curse from a religious saint, so how can she be cured by the blessings of a religious saint? Had she fallen sick due to some curse, perhaps she could have been cured by some blessing."

He said, "You can say whatever you like, but this case is a puzzle. What you are saying makes sense, but if you know of some saint or monk, please let me know."

I said, "In that case I do know many saints and monks. I will take you to some."

One of my friends used to live nearby in the hills – some ten or twelve miles away. He was not a saint or monk, but he was a carefree, easygoing man. He had earned enough money for himself and he lived easily on the interest of it. He had built a small hut in the hills and he lived there alone, ecstatically.

I said to him, "You have to become a saint for one day."

He asked, "What do you mean?"

I said, "You just have to smear ash all over your body and sit near a holy bonfire wearing only a tiny piece of loincloth."

"Oh?" he replied. "What nonsense are you talking? For what? Is there going to be some film shooting, or what?"

I said, "There is a poor doctor whose wife is dying. He needs the blessings of some saint or monk. Just pick up some ash, give it to him saying, 'Go! Everything will be alright.'"

He started saying, "You are putting me in a great difficulty. Everyone in this village knows me – even that doctor knows me."

I said, "He knows you but before he comes I will bring a barber to you and have you faked as a real saint – so much so that even if a film shooting were to take place, in that moment there would be no problem."

He said, "All this doesn't feel right. And after this you will be gone, but I won't be able to even enter the village. People will ask, 'What happened? Did your father die? Why have you shaved your head? And oh, what has happened to your mustache?' There is great respect around here for my mustache." He truly possessed a very splendid mustache and he used to keep it well waxed and twirled.

I said, "Whatever happens, his wife has to be saved. The mustache will grow back again, but how would this poor man ever bring back his wife?"

I only managed to get him to agree to the act with great difficulty. I got his head shaved, his mustache shaved. He went on cursing me and I went on getting him shaved as two men held him down by both his arms. Getting the mustache shaved was really difficult. We got him to take off his normal clothes, but he stubbornly stopped at his underwear. I told him that an enlightened saint also drops his underwear and that: "I have already told the doctor that you are an enlightened saint."

He said, "This is a great torture. And I have nothing to do with all of this!"

I made him sit, waiting. It was winter, but because of the bonfire there was some relief for the poor fellow. Upon his arrival the doctor fell prostrate at his feet. He didn't even bother to look up to see who this fellow was. The doctor held his feet saying, "Save us!" And my friend must have thought that when the matter had come this far then why not complete the whole act, so he said, "Don't be afraid, my son! Get up. Is there some trouble with your wife?"

The doctor said, "I am a doctor, but first I always have to inquire of the patient what kind of ailment he or she has, and here are you sitting miles away and you see that my wife has some sickness. I have tried all sorts of treatments..."

The saint said, "But to no avail. And it will not be of any use because the sickness is spiritual and you are caught up in physical treatment. Here, take this ash: first you eat it, then..."

The doctor interrupted, "But it is my wife who is sick, not me."

The saint said, "Shut up! It is because of your wrongdoings that your wife is sick. First you must eat the ash and then take the remainder to your wife. And if there are children in the home, distribute it amongst them also. Everything will be alright."

I had gone with him. I was watching all this, standing there. I saw the doctor eating the ash, and I also saw him take it home.

But is there ever a wife cured by ash? She was going to die and that she did. In fact, before we could reach back home she was dead.

The doctor said, "What kind of a saint is that fellow? That evil guy made me eat the ash as well, and added to that, he killed my wife."

I said, "Only saints can understand the miracles of saints. You will not. Practice your medicine. Your wife has gone to heaven."

He said, "This is a strange situation. What kind of a saint did you take me to? First he made me eat the ash – that was not right and

I became a little suspicious then and there – and that suspicion proved right. And that idiot even said to me that it is because of *my* wrongdoings that my wife is dying!"

I said, "Don't be in a panic. It is you who was in such a great search for some saint or monk. It was only with much difficulty that I could find one – you have no idea how much trouble I went to. First, make your second marriage, then I will tell you all about it."

In India there are engineers, there are doctors, architects and scientists, but it all remains only on the intellectual level. The centuries-old conditioning lying within them is as tight around them as chains. People go to the West and then return after being educated there, but still the same tangle of old conditioning remains. And people praise them highly for still being in that tangle: "Look, he has been to the West, he has been educated in the Western universities, and yet he has not abandoned his Indianness. He still goes to the temple. He still visits the mosque. He still bows down to his holy scriptures first thing in the morning after waking up and before starting any other activity."

This country can certainly be taken into the twenty-first century, but before that it has to be freed from thousands of years of old conditioning. And there is only one way to be freed of this and I am continuously talking only of that: that if in some way you can learn to meditate, that if in some way you can learn to create that space within you where the waves of thoughts cease – where there remains no commotion, no thinking, no nothing; where you become peaceful, serene, and silent – in that silence you are disconnected from the past and you arrive in the present. And someone who has arrived into the present can proceed on the journey of tomorrow, but first he will have to be brought into the present.

India, as yet, is not in the present. Its eyes are focused on the past, its revered figures are in the past, its golden age is in the past. All these circumstances will have to be changed.

I have heard…

A lean young man was racing on a motorbike on a road. The wind was strong from the opposite direction. He stopped the bike and changed his coat to face backward, so that the wind would not affect his chest too much and he wouldn't catch cold. Putting the coat on backward, he buttoned it up, tightened his muffler on his neck and took off again.

A Sirdarji was coming from the opposite direction and seeing the young man he said, "My God! This man is sitting on the bike facing backward and is going so fast!" It was so unnerving that in the confusion of it all he collided with the young man. The young man fell off his motorbike and fell unconscious. The Sirdarji thought to himself, "What sort of trouble have I got myself into? Moreover what kind of fellow is this young man? And now I must straighten his neck. There is no one else around whom I can call for help."

So he gave a big jerk to the young man's neck and said, "Victory to the guru! Victory to the path of the guru!" With yet another mighty jerk he turned the face of the young man in the "right" direction.

By this time the police van had arrived and an officer asked him what the matter was.

The Sirdar said, "The matter? This young man was sitting on the motorbike facing in the wrong direction."

The policeman said, "Is he alive?"

Sirdarji said, "He was alive, but he is a strange kind of man! As long as his head was facing in the wrong direction he was alive. With much difficulty and with the grace of the guruji I have straightened his neck into the right direction – but now he is not breathing. Could you take over and look after this breathing business. I have to go…"

The policeman looked closely to see what the situation was. The Sirdar's statement seemed to be correct. The buttons of the man's coat supported his story. By the time the policeman undid the buttons and discovered that the young man had been wearing the coat back to front, the Sirdarji was gone.

The young fellow was unnecessarily killed.

The condition of India is something like this too. You are not facing the direction in which you are going. You are facing where you have come from. If you keep falling into ditches again and again, it is no wonder.

Look toward the future. You have looked for long enough through your past, and nothing at all has come into your hands: your hands are empty, your stomach is empty: your poverty goes on increasing. Look toward the future and conditions will start changing. You have no lack of genius but you have been using it in a wrong dimension, in a wrong direction. Give it the right direction.

And my experience is that if you can experience meditation even for a short while during twenty-four hours, if you can be bathed in it, become fresh, then you will arrive in the present – exactly at the place where you are. And it is from here that the path to the future proceeds.

So whether it is about the twenty-first century or the twenty-second century, the path to the future proceeds from *here*. But those politicians who are saying to you that the future – the twenty-first century – is to be ushered in, are not even here themselves. The twenty-first century is far away. Even the twentieth century has not come to them.

You can go and see this in Delhi. All sorts of astrologers, palmists, all manner of monks and saints and gurus are sitting there, thoroughly at home. Each politician has some saint as his guru. There is always one palmist or another who will read the lines on his palm and tell him when to fill in his nomination form, when the stars are favorable and when they are not.

One friend of mine was a very old member of parliament. He was called "the father of the parliament." I used to stay at his place, but to be his guest was always trouble. He was the friend of my father – he was old – and the trouble was he would not allow me to leave until his astrologer had tallied all the charts and maps and declared when the right time for traveling was. If the train was to leave at eleven that day, he would wake me up early and already bring me to the railway station at six in the morning.

I would say, "This is beyond all understanding."

And he would say, "Six o'clock is the astrologically correct time for departure. The train may come at any time it wants, but the house must be left at six if you want an auspicious outcome from the journey. Otherwise there will be ill-effects, and then what will I tell your father?"

I would think how much trouble this was. And if he would just leave me there and return home – but no, no way. He would sit there and bend my ear talking from six in the morning until the train came. And no train ever comes on time in this country...

Only once have I ever seen a train coming on time, even though I have been continuously traveling on them in this country for thirty years, to every nook and corner of the country. But only once! So then I had gone to thank the driver, that it was a blessed occasion in my life: "For once you have brought the train in at the right time, down to the very last second."

The driver said, "Before thanking me, kindly listen. In fact, this is yesterday's train, twenty-four hours late."

I said, "I thought I was to have that one experience – but no." And I asked the driver, "Why do you unnecessarily bother to publish railway timetables when the trains come when they want to come?"

The station master was standing next to us. He said to me, "Don't mention the timetable!"

I said, "Why?"

He said, "If we did not publish the timetable, how would we know how late each train is running? Do you want to put us in even more of a mess? What is the purpose of a timetable? – one comes to know whether a train is late by twelve hours or fourteen hours or twenty-four hours. Otherwise, one will not even know when a train came, when it left, where it left to, did it even leave at all or not? The timetable must be published."

I said, "Alright my friend, let it be published."

My parliamentarian friend had turned seventy years old, and in his mind he had great ideas for solving great problems. He introduced me to Jugal Kishore Birla in the hope that if Birla were to become interested in what I was saying there would be no shortage of money for my work – that he would financially support any work I might be doing.

Birla said, "There are only two things worth doing. One is *Go-raksha*, protecting the cow."

I thought to myself, "I am finished! I am not here to do *Go-raksha*: keep your money to yourself. Here, the whole of humanity is approaching death and there are people whose eyes are focused backwards saying, '*Go-raksha*!'"

"And the second thing," he said, "is to spread the Hindu religion. Then, you can have as much money as you want. I am ready to give a blank check."

I said, "You can keep that checkbook. I can spread religion, but not the Hindu religion, because the moment religion becomes Hindu, it is no longer religion. The moment it becomes Mohammedan, it is no longer religion. The moment it becomes Christian, it is no longer religion. Religion is religion only as long as there is no adjective to it. Before you put an adjective on it, religion is a fragrance in the open sky, it is the light of the stars in an unclouded sky."

You see a bird flying in the sky and your heart is overjoyed by its beauty, and then you put this same bird in a golden cage hanging in your house… Perhaps you may think it is still the same bird – you are mistaken. It is not the same bird. That bird had the whole sky; this bird has nothing except a cage. That bird was alive; this bird is alive only in name – it is "alive" because it breathes. What aliveness has a bird whose wings have no freedom?

Religion is a free state, like a bird on the wing in the sky.

So I said to Jugal Kishore Birla, "I will talk of religion my whole life – until the last breath of my life, but I will not allow any adjective to settle over it. An adjective settles and the thing is dead, an adjective comes and the bird is encaged!"

He said, "I have nothing to do with religion, I want just the *sanatan dharma* – the Hindu religion."

I said, "Keep your *sanatan dharma* with you, as well as your checkbook."

The people with whom this country has identified over the centuries...anyone threatening that identification will feel like an enemy. So because of this, who knows if people, even unknowingly, start taking me as an enemy. I embark on taking them out of their cages, and they cover my hands with blood. They are not ready to come out of the cage.

Who will take this country into the twenty-first century? The politicians? No. But they pass on a good dream to you: they are dealers in dreams. They give you dreams and take a cash vote from you, but those dreams never materialize. In five years' time you will have forgotten all about them and then again new dealers of dreams will arrive. Then again you will vote in the hope that perhaps what couldn't happen yesterday may happen today.

But politics has never allowed man to grow. Politics simply doesn't want man to grow, because the more developed a man is the more difficult it becomes to enslave him, the more difficult it becomes to stop him from becoming free, the more difficult it is to make him obedient.

Freedom is revolution. It is only revolution that can take you into the future – a spiritual revolution. And the key to that revolution is meditation.

Osho,
You must already know that in India the game of cricket is so popular that people become crazy over it. Because this foreign game is so prevalent, several of India's own games don't get a chance to come to the forefront. It has reached the point where the test players in cricket – and I don't want to mention anybody by name – are worshipped in India, are taken as stars. But because of this game several of India's own games haven't been able to prosper. How do you look at this craze?

A craze is a craze, whether it is in India or outside India. In the world different games turn people crazy, but their purpose is one. In

California last year the University of California did a survey for the whole year on one thing: how people go absolutely crazy whenever there are soccer matches. And for seven days after the matches the crime rate remains up by fourteen percent. There is more violence, more suicide, more rape – and yet the government allows those games to continue.

Those games cannot be stopped, and I also would not say that they should be, because if the madness that gets released from people through playing those games didn't happen, then there would be even more rapes, even more violence. No matter what the game – cricket, football, volleyball, hockey or whatever – all are refined methods for releasing your violence. And as long as there is violence in man, anger in man, I see no harm in these games. I don't think that I have any objection if people revere the cricket players like they do the political leaders or film stars. My only concern is that the place of the political leaders should be at the very bottom.

Film stars are helpful in allowing the repressed love and repressed emotions that are within people to be released – they should get respect. But the misfortune that has happened in the recent past is that film actors are becoming intoxicated by the idea of getting into politics. This is a fall. This is not building on their respect. When they were film actors they were artists. Now, now there is no art in their life. They should go back. The only people to be sent into politics should be those who are incapable of doing anything else whatsoever, because there they have nothing to do.

Even cricket players, or football players or the players of other games, help release things from within you. Seeing them play, many emotions from within you are also released.

As far as Indian games are concerned, there is not one amongst them which can stand alongside cricket or football or hockey. And that is no one's fault. For example, no matter how much you say "kabaddi-kabaddi-kabaddi...," No one enjoys it at all. People are doing "kabaddi-kabaddi" everyday in their homes – husband with wife. The whole country has become a kabaddi playground. Now do you want more kabaddi happening here? And who will be interested in it? You are already doing it at home. Now who is going to go to watch it at the playground? Or *gilli-danda*...?

There is no substance in Indian games. Now this is the helpless reality. What can anyone do about it? And there is a reason why there is no grit in these Indian games – everything has a reason behind it.

Indian games are children's games. In India, no one ever had a youth because we married the children too young. My mother is present here. She was married at the age of seven. My father may have been some twelve years of age. If one is married at the age of twelve, will he then worry about the affairs of the home or will he play football and cricket?

Indian games are the games of the small children. Western games are games of youth.

The age of youth came in the West because there, the age of marriage kept going up. Now people there marry at the age of twenty-five, twenty-six, thirty years of age. A young person reaches a marriageable age at fourteen. Energy and power arise within him – now he can give birth to children. Girls become capable of becoming mothers at the age of thirteen, but in the West they will wait for another fifteen years. These fifteen years of youth need to be released somewhere, hence Western games are the games of youth – and their flavor is different.

Indian games are the rattles of small children. Now if you unnecessarily carry them around on your head because they are Indian, that is your choice. Indians don't have a single game born from the age of youth.

And you should take this into account, that games also have an age. A country where people live longer, there, some other games also become more important – for example, chess. These are the games of the old, not of the young. These are the games of those to whom nothing else is left to do. They have done everything. Only one idiocy is left and they should do this too – and then the time has come for their release from this world. After that release there is neither *kabaddi* nor chess. Games too have their age. In a country where the average age is younger, such games of old age don't have a great appeal or wide prevalence.

But I would like to say this: if people give respect to someone because of playing games or respect to someone because of acting or because of music... For example, the Beatles received great respect throughout the world. The music was not something great but it belonged to the youth. It was not classical. For classical music you need old age; a time, a long time, is needed to understand classical music. The Beatles and the other musicians after them in the West were all simply jumping up and down. It was neither dance nor music, but all the youth needed it. Through that jumping up and down their emotions were released. Otherwise these same emotions would have led to crime.

There should be arrangements in every school for people's emotions to be given outlets. Now there is a problem in our country: students go on strike, they throw stones, they harass teachers and set schools on fire. But we are responsible for this. We do not provide appropriate ways for their emotions to be released. Before they throw a stone, these same hands that throw a stone and feel a kind of relief, can play volleyball. They will get the same relief through volleyball and the windows panes of the school will be safe too. The walls of the school and the teachers of the school will all be safe.

There is a psychology of games, and the psychology is that the emotions repressed within us flow away through them and we become a bit lighter inside.

It is not that the Western games are stopping Indian games from advancing. India just doesn't have the games of the youth, because youth is a very, very new arrival to India. That too has come through the West – through their system of education – and hence we copy their games too.

India only has the games of small children. Those games cannot be taken to such complexity that you can make a person a star, a hero – that he is very skilled in playing gilli-danda. People will only laugh when they see him: "Hey smart guy! Is there nothing else for you as a pastime? Gilli-danda? Let the small children play it. Find something else to do."

There is no question of India in it. The question in it is of age and of different age groups.

For centuries in India we have not allowed youth to have a place, hence many things of youth have simply never developed in India. Small children were married, so there never arose the question of love marriages. From where could that question arise? The question of love marriages can only arise if we do not arrange the marriages of small children, and allow them to attain to youth – and allow the love energy to arise in them and allow them the opportunity for men and women to mix. Then the question of love marriages can arise.

Here in India children were married at such an early age that the husband and the wife grew up together like brother and sister. The sanskrit word *bhagini* is ancient. It has two meanings: both "the wife" and "the sister." It's a lovely word. It is indicative of the fact that the marriages used to take place at such an early age that the couple were not even aware that there is something like the relationship of a husband and wife – at the most, brother and sister. Just as there were other brothers and sisters in the house, one more sister had joined the family. They would grow up together, they would grow into youth together. There was never the chance to go to the beach or down the lovers' lanes, because this sister was a permanent beach or lovers' lane – tied to you. There were other brothers as well at this "beach," but they had their own sisters with them.

For thousands of years we did not allow youth to happen. And along with this, when the boy was six, seven or eight years of age, he would join the parents in their profession. He would start going to the fields with the parents, start helping in their carpentry, in their shoe-making, he would start sitting in their shop. He would just do some little things, helping the parents. He wouldn't even notice that any period of youth came or went. Between his childhood and his old age there was no place, no room for any youth.

Youth is the outcome of the modern education that came from the West. And it is good that it came, because it gave birth to a new class – the youth – and it gave birth to new colors and new forms of this youth. The games of youth will be their own, the literature of youth will be their own, the movies of youth will be their own, the songs of youth will be their own. A whole new dimension has opened up that is altogether new. And just because it has come from the West and we have nothing parallel to it before, don't think that it has suppressed anything. It has suppressed nothing. A vacuum has been created and into that vacuum has come that which was only available from the West.

For example, we have never made any scientific discoveries in this country. Whatever science comes, it is coming from the West. Whatever is good or bad and accompanies that science will also come from the West. Don't say that it has come after suppressing something of yours. We simply didn't have anything – in the realms of "science" we were empty and vacant. Science comes from the West.

And everything has two sides: a good side and a bad side.

For example, birth control came from the West, meaning that a couple can have a child if they want one or not. Now its positive outcome can be that we can reduce the population of the country and increase prosperity. And the other outcome may be that we can fill the whole country with prostitutes and destroy the whole moral order of the country, because now you cannot find out if your wife has been intimate with the neighbor, now you cannot simply confirm that this son is, in fact, yours.

All this is in our hands. Science in itself is neutral – how we make use of it will depend on us.

These games are also neutral – how we use them will also depend on us. And we should develop the approach of making a right use of everything. Everything can be used in such a way that the innermost soul of this country, that is suppressed under the rubbish of thousands of years, can be washed clean.

CHAPTER 10

THE
TREASURE
OF ONE'S OWN EXPERIENCE

Osho,
Expression of thought and freedom of speech are the basic
foundations of democracy. Anyone is free to agree with or
oppose your statements. But as it is, people oppose you and they
do not want to give you the freedom to carry on with your work.
Why is this so?

The same cup destroyed the illusions of both:
The drunkards went to the mosque, the priest to the pub.

If you open your eyes and see just how much illusion and how much
reality resides in what we call life and all the values we are so proud
of, you can't help but be shocked.

Such lies have been propagated in the name of democracy, and
for so long in this world, that we miss the point that there is a need to
rethink their reality. It is said that democracy is "of the people, by the
people and for the people" – and even such a great lie starts to appear
as truth after having been repeated so many times.

Adolf Hitler used to say: "I have found only one difference between truth and lies, and that is of repetition. A lie is a new truth that
has not yet been repeated and truth is an old lie – traditional – that has
been repeated for centuries, generation after generation."

There is an element of some truth in his statement, because in no
country is there a government "of the people, by the people, for the
people." And these lies are very lovely, very sweet – but they are
certainly poisonous. And although they are poisonous, hundreds of
millions of people drink them very happily. And those who publicize

these lies as truths, rule. They are the government: the government is for them, the government is by them – although they say that they are the servants of the people.

But it is a very strange world. Here, the people called "the servants of the people" are sitting over the people as if they are the masters. Yes, of course they are required to repeat the lie once again after five years; once again they must come to the doors of people and say, "We are your servants." Once your vote is cast in his favor, this same person who had come to you like a beggar...even the door man at his office will not let you in. You will not even be allowed to meet the man!

This is a strange kind of service to the people. The people are dying of hunger – every day the people go on falling into more and more discomfort and suffering – but the servants of this same public are living in luxury. Let them live in enjoyment and pleasures, let them have their revelry. My objection is not about that. My objection is about their lies.

You have said, "Expression of thought and freedom of speech are the basic foundations of democracy..."

And the experience of my entire life says that there is no "freedom of thought" anywhere. I have just returned from a trip around the world. There is not one single country on this earth where you are free to say exactly what has arisen in your heart. You are supposed to say what people want to hear. Many countries wanted me to become a resident of their country, since they felt that thousands upon thousands of sannyasins would come there because of me and their country would benefit financially. They had no interest in me. Their interest was that because of those thousands of visitors, the wealth of their country would grow. But they all had conditions for me, and the surprising thing is that the conditions of all of them were the same. Every country had the condition: "We would be very happy if you stayed here, but you should not say anything against the government and you should not say anything against the religion of our country. Just these two things. If you can fulfill these two conditions, you are welcome."

The same is the situation in this country, India. My whole life I have been receiving summons from the government offices, from the courts; orders to be present in the court because someone has filed a case against me because I have said something that has hurt that man's religious feelings. This is a very interesting matter. Your religious feeling is so weak, so spineless, that someone says something against it and it is hurt. Throw away such spineless and rubbishy feelings! Your inner religiousness should be of steel. What kind of rotten and worthless religiousness are you carrying?

Any person who goes to court saying that his religious feelings are hurt should be sued by the court: "Do you have such weak feelings? Can't you find some vital and healthy philosophy of life? Can't you find a system of thought which no one can hurt?"

To date I have never said to any court that my religious feelings are hurt. I am, in fact, waiting for the man who can hurt my religious feelings. I have wandered the whole world inviting such a person who can come and hurt my religious feelings. My religious feeling is my own experience. How can you hurt it?

But people have borrowed stale religious feelings that belong to others. They are not their own. Someone has whispered an initiation mantra in their ears – a guru-mantra, the mantra given by some so-called religious teacher – and on these borrowed and stale things, on this sand, they have built their palaces. Give a slight push and their palaces will begin to crumble, their palaces will begin to shake. But the mistake here is not of the one who gives the push. If you build your palace on sand, whose mistake is it? If you draw lines on water and they disappear, who is responsible?

And if it is true that to speak against someone's religion, someone's philosophy, is a crime, then Krishna has also committed this crime, Buddha has also committed this crime, Jesus has also committed this crime, Mohammed has also committed this crime – and Kabir, and Nanak. All the thinkers who have been in this world have committed a crime, a serious crime, because they have ruthlessly destroyed what was wrong. And those who have been attached to these wrongs must certainly have been hurt.

If no Kabirs are being born today in the world, if no Gautam Buddhas are being born today in the world, your democracy is responsible for it.

It is strange. In democracy, there should be a Kabir in every village, there should be a Nanak in every house, a Socrates and a Mansoor in every place, because the very foundation of democracy is freedom of thought. When there was no democracy in the world and there was no freedom of thought, this world touched great heights. And now? Now, it is a crime to fly to the heights in this world, your wings will be cut – because your flying to the heights hurts the hearts of those who are sitting in the dark valleys.

Democracy could have been a marvelous experience in the evolution of man's soul. But it was not to be so. What has happened is just the opposite: "Much bleating but little wool" – very lofty, great words and an ugly reality behind it.

There is no freedom of thought anywhere, but every person should dare to have freedom of thought. This is inviting trouble, this is inviting it on oneself, but this trouble is worth inviting, because it is by passing through this challenge that a sharpness will come into your life, that a shine will enter your intelligence, that a luminosity will come into your being. Whereas carrying the whole load of other people's most beautiful ideas, you are only a donkey loaded with the Gita, the Koran and the Bible – carrying them, but still a donkey. Don't start thinking: "All the religious scriptures are loaded on my back, so what more is needed? Before long angels must be waiting to welcome me at the gates of heaven with harps..."

Even a small experience of your own, even a small thought born out of your own experience – a tiny seed will fill your life with more flowers than you can ever imagine.

Have you ever paid attention to what a potential a tiny seed has? A small seed can fill the whole earth with flowers – but the seed should be an alive one.

A thought is alive when it is born out of your own being, when your own heartbeat is in it, when it is sustained by the circulation of your own blood, when your own breath breathes through it.

My lifelong effort has been to shake you, to nudge you, to say to you: "How long are you going to remain filled with these borrowed, stale thoughts? Be ashamed! Enough of shamelessness! Let there be something of your own. Let there be some treasure of your own. And in this life there is no greater treasure than the treasure of experience – one's own experience.

There is a sweet story on this line.

Buddha has come to a village.

And those days were beautiful; those were the days when this country witnessed the Everest of consciousness. This country has never climbed mountains but it has touched the highest of peaks of consciousness.

Buddha is coming to a village. The young king of that land's old prime minister says to him, "You should go to welcome Buddha. The whole village is going to welcome him, and it will be very insulting of us if Buddha comes to the village and the king does not go to welcome him."

The king said, "What sort of topsy-turvy notions do you have? Have you gone crazy in your old age? I am a king; Buddha is a beggar. If he wants to meet me he will have to come to my doors. For what possible reason should I go to welcome him?"

There were tears in the eyes of the old man and he said, "Please accept my resignation. Now, I won't be able to work for you. It is no good working for such a small person."

The old man was badly needed. He was the wisest man in the kingdom. The king couldn't afford to lose him. He said, "You are mad to be ready to resign over such a petty matter."

The old prime minister said, "Either you have to walk on foot to Buddha and bow down at his feet or my resignation is unavoidable. When people hear, what will they say? That the king of our land doesn't even have this much understanding: that when an awakened one – one illumined by his own light, one fragrant with his own fragrance – is in the village he can't walk a few steps to greet him. What do you have anyway? Wealth and the kingdom – and because of these you think that you are a king, and that Buddha is a beggar. You shouldn't forget that this man was also a king before – and a greater one for that matter, and one that had everything. His kingdom was bigger than yours and he left that kingdom behind. His being a beggar has a far higher status than his being a king. It is one rung further up the ladder. He is no ordinary beggar. He is a king who dropped his kingdom just like that. You are still far away from that."

The king had to go. There was truth in the statements of the prime minister. The king bowed down at Buddha's feet. Buddha even said, "You unnecessarily took the trouble. I was coming myself – my route passed by the side of your palace. Moreover, I am just a beggar and you are a king."

But it was upon seeing Buddha that the king became aware that sometimes this too can happen – that a beggar is a king and a king a beggar.

You may have everything on the outside, but if you have no inner experience of your own, if no lamp is lit within you, if your inner lamps are still unlit… On the outside it may be Diwali, the festival of lights, for you, but you are still much poorer than the person within whom even one single lamp is lit – even if on the outside it may be a moonless night for him.

There should be freedom of thought, but nobody will give it to you. You will have to claim it. Drop the illusion that if you called your constitution "a democratic constitution," you will have freedom of thought. What on earth will you think? Even if you have freedom of thought, what will you think? What you are reading in the news-papers is what will circulate in your mind.

For freedom of thought, a guarantee of freedom in the constitu-tion is not enough. Freedom of thought is a very unique experiment. First of all you will have to become free of thoughts, because right now all the thoughts you have belong to others. First you will have to remove this rubbish of others' thoughts from your mind.

This is what we have called dhyana, meditation, in this country.

Meditation means freedom from others' thoughts. And then you become a blank paper, a plain, innocent child's mind, which has no writing on it. And then from your innermost being start arising, wak-ing, flowering, those thoughts that are called free thoughts. They do not come from the outside; they grow from within you. And when you have your own thoughts, then whether the governments talk of democracy or not, your thoughts will give you that much courage and strength that you can encounter the greatest of governments.

The power of one's own thoughts is not smaller than any nuclear bomb. Rather it is more. After all, the nuclear bomb is the child of man's thoughts too – a child of those people's thoughts who could think for themselves. Its potentiality cannot be more than the potentiality of thoughts; it is, after all, the child of thoughts.

Democracy will be born the day meditation spreads all over the world. Without the thread of meditation spreading everywhere democracy is not possible. You may talk a millionfold about freedom, and about freedom of thought, but you just don't have the capability to think freely. Hence, I want to teach you a science from its fundamental roots so that whether democracy comes into the world or not, at least within yourself comes freedom. And if the lamp is lit in one person, then from this lamp it becomes very easy for other lamps in other people to be lit.

One is not to pass on thoughts to others. If you can pass on meditation to others, then you have shared some love, some compassion; then you have given something worth giving. Then, thoughts will be born within the person of their own accord.

Democracy has failed in the whole world because its very first step has not been fulfilled. The first step is the thread of meditation. Meditation – and only meditation – gives birth to that shine in your eyes, that depth and intensity in your eyes, that sharpness in your vision, which cuts through all lies and uncovers and finds the truth – even if it is hidden under a million layers. And if thousands of people can become adept in meditation, there will be freedom of thought in the world. Out of that freedom of thought, democracy will be born.

No freedom of thought can be born out of democracy. Who will give birth to it? Worthless politicians create your constitution, then these same worthless politicians suck your blood in the name of democracy. It is a strange game that is going on in the world. You are being "served." The old proverb is quite right: "He who serves receives rich dividends." In search of that rich dividend people are willing even "to serve."

I have heard that a politician was contesting an election. He was going door-to-door telling people: "It is election-time, and I earnestly hope I can count on your vote."

One woman was taking a walk in the garden with five or six children. He kissed all the children, and asked the woman: "Remember me. Please do not forget me. And your children are very beautiful and lovely."

The woman said, "Excuse me, I am their nursemaid, not their mother."

The politician said, "Damn it! I unnecessarily kissed these fools. And their noses are running and whatnot!

"All sorts of things have to be done to get votes. But you are quite a woman! Why didn't you tell me earlier that you are only a nursemaid and they're not your children? And you are an amazing nursemaid to have six children drenched with runny noses! But stay here. Other candidates are following me. Let each of them kiss the children. When they have all been kissed at least the runny noses will have been wiped clean!"

There is a joke about the American president, Mr. Hoover....

There are many North American Indians in America, to whom America actually belongs. It is very interesting. America is called "the greatest democracy in the world" and those poor North American Indians to whom America really belongs have been imprisoned in forest reserves. And not one of those who is ruling America, is American.

This was their anger with me, because I had challenged the president of America "If you take me to be a foreigner...I have been a foreigner only for five years, but you and your forefathers have been foreigners for three hundred years. Now tell us, who is more of a foreigner? And I am not an invader. You and your forefathers are invaders. If anybody has committed a crime, it is you."

And the people to whom the country belongs, these so-called Americans, have played such cunning games with the North American Indians that you cannot imagine. The Indians have been divided into small groups and kept in forest settlements. And each person is given such a large pension that they do not demand work and so they do not need to come to the cities. You can go around the whole of America and you will not even notice the actual natives of America. These people to whom the country belongs are lying drunk in the forests – because they are getting free money in a pension. They gamble, become drunkards, become hooligans, indulge in fights, end up in jails – what else can they do? When someone is getting free money, what else is he going to do? Manipulated through the power of money, you will find them drunk, locked up in jails, caught up in crimes – the rightful owners of the country. And this is "the greatest free country, the greatest democratic country"!

So this joke about President Hoover has been in vogue.

It is his election time and he has gone to a North American Indian Reserve to solicit votes – just as the politicians the world over are known to do. He says, "If you elect me, I will have schools opened here."

And all the Indians say in unison, "Hoo-hoo!" and there is a peal of laughter.

Hoover is encouraged. "And we will open a hospital here."

The Indians say, "Hoo-hoo!" and a peal of laughter follows.

With this Mr. Hoover goes on, feeling encouraged, "Don't worry. If I become the president, I will even get a university opened here."

And they say, "Hoo-hoo!" They clap, they laugh loudly, and say, "Hoo-hoo!"

Hoover is very happy. By the time he leaves the meeting he is so impressed that he asks the Indian chief to take him around the village so that he can familiarize himself with the area, because "there is so much to be done for this place and your people. And what wonderful people you all are!"

The chief says, "Everything is fine. I have no objection to taking you around, but these people have a very bad habit. They will just sit down anywhere and deposit hoo-hoo."

Hoover says, "Deposit hoo-hoo?"

The chief says, "Look! Wherever on the pathways you look you will see piles of hoo-hoo."

Hoover says, "This is too much! Those wretched fellows! When I was promising them one thing after another at the top of my voice and they were laughing and 'hoo-hoo-ing...' Only now I understand what they meant. I thought those bastards had picked up the first part of my name, Hoover, and were rejoicing with it."

The chief answers, "What can I say to you? Every politician promises these same things, and every time the same thing happens – again and again. No schools open anywhere and the politician is never seen again. And these are simple people. They have understood that all these talks are hoo-hoo. There is no substance in them, or only as much as in hoo-hoo. So please don't get annoyed. They don't hoo-hoo only you. Whenever any politician comes here to lecture, these fellows will clap and shout, 'Hoo-hoo!' Whoever hears their 'Hoo-hoo' is pleased, thinking they are shouting praises in their own language, but in fact it is their dirtiest abuse."

Democracy will not descend from the heavens.

You may write it down in your laws, you may discuss it in your constitutions, but democracy will not descend from the heavens, otherwise it would have descended by now. I want to say to you that if democracy ever comes, there is only one route for it: it will come from within you. When hundreds of millions of people have developed the capacity for free thinking, then a collective expression of that capacity – the ultimate outcome of that capacity – will be democracy.

So, instead of saying that the foundation stone of freedom of thought has been placed in democracy, it would be more correct to say that if you develop the capacity for free thinking, the foundation stone of democracy can be laid. Free thinking is a million times more precious than democracy; democracy is but a small outcome of free thinking. There will be thousands of other outcomes as well.

The greatest outcome will be that you will arrive at godliness. The smallest outcome will be that around you democracy will be created. The power of free thought is infinite, but before that, it is necessary that you have arrived to that health called meditation.

CHAPTER 11

THE
ROOTS
OF TERRORISM

Osho,
Today the threat of terrorism haunts the whole world. What
are the origins of this sickness and insanity in man? What is
the diagnosis and what is the remedy for it? Can it be hoped
that one day mankind can be free of terrorism?

If mankind was only just beginning to be haunted by terrorism, things would be very easy. But mankind has always been haunted by terrorism, hence the matter is very complex. The forms of terrorism have changed – this insanity has been taking on newer and newer colors, newer and newer forms – but in the whole history of mankind, except for a few people who can be counted on the fingers of two hands, all the remaining people have been sick in one way or another. These sicknesses are as old as man himself, and that is why whenever someone has tried to eliminate these sicknesses, these insanities, insane humanity has eliminated the very man himself.

The people who poisoned Socrates and who put Jesus on the cross are proof of it. What Socrates was saying was providing the right diagnosis in order to make man healthy again, but the crowd does not want to accept that it is insane. And any man who wants to become healthy has first to accept this much: that he is not healthy. This is where the difficulty comes in.

There are thousands of madhouses in the world, but there is not a single madman ready to accept that he is mad. Every madman tries to prove that the whole world may be mad, but he is not. The people in whose lives an inner revolution has taken place, who have become transformed, are that very handful of people who have accepted that they were insane, that they were sick, that they were restless.

The first step toward a healthy life is to accept one's state of unhealthiness.

But if someone says to you that you are beautiful, it feels very good, and if someone says that you are not beautiful, it feels very bad. If someone says to you that you are right, it feels good, it reassures, it consoles. And if someone exposes your wounds to you, that man seems like the enemy.

The causes of man's unhealthiness are very clear-cut. First of all, man has made unnaturalness the goal of life instead of the natural. Our eyes are focused on the unnatural instead of on the natural. The more unnatural a man becomes, the more we respect him: he is a sadhu, a saint, a great soul, a siddha. Our respect inspires him to become even more unnatural, and our respect becomes a thirst within us to follow him also, to follow in his footsteps, because we see that the whole world is giving this man respect: "I may be wrong, but the whole world cannot be wrong."

Everybody thinks like this and in this way that which is wrong goes on being worshipped. Fallacies go on being respected, unnaturalnesses are revered, and we get caught in the net. If somebody practices fasting, he receives our respect – as if dying from hunger has anything to do with spirituality. If that were so, all the starving people of the world would be spiritual. But someone becomes spiritual neither by starving himself nor through excessive eating. A balance, an equilibrium, is needed in life. Life is like walking on a razor's edge – even the slightest movement this way or that, and you are in trouble!

The key for becoming healthy is right balance – an awareness that nothing in life gets taken to extremes. Extremity is sickness. But go and look at the writings of all the religions, try to understand the history of all the religions, and you will find that extremity is revered everywhere. A person who is ordinary, simple – nobody bothers about him. There is no respect for ordinariness. In this world, there is worship for the extraordinary, respect for the extraordinary. And in order to be extraordinary, it is necessary to go to extremes.

This humanity that you are seeing as insane, and this terrorism that is overshadowing the whole world, is the result of centuries of extremity. A man stands naked under the hot sun or in the cold, and you give respect to him. In the deserts of Arabia where the sun blazes like fire and the sand burns like fire, there, in that terrifying heat, the Sufis keep themselves covered in woolen blankets. They get respect. You may be surprised to know that the very word Sufi has come out of the root *suf*, wool. Suf means wool; he who keeps himself covered in woolen blanket is a Sufi.

And this is very interesting: when you worship madness, you are giving an indication that you yourself would like to live that madness too. It is another matter that today you yourself are helpless, it is another matter that today you do not have so much courage, it is another matter that today the circumstances are not in your favor. So never mind – tomorrow, in your next life! But your reverence indicates the direction of your life and your inner desire.

A simple man, an ordinary man in whose life there are no extremes will not even be noticed by you. Your eyes will miss him – and he is the healthy one. He will be in bliss, in peace, carefree – but not respected.

I will say it another way: we have to change our values around giving respect. We have given too much respect to egoists. And the ways of the ego are very subtle, and there is no bigger disease than the ego. But we feed our own children with this poison from their very childhood – although what we do is out of love, there is nothing wrong in our intentions. I do not suspect your intentions, but we feed them poison unknowingly.

Every father wants his son to be top of the class, top of the university, become famous all over the country; receive national honors such as Padmabhooshan, Bharat Ratna; become a Nobel Prize winner. But nobody thinks that in the family, in school, in the neighborhood, all around, respect is given to the egoist – someone who is in front. Then this race, this fever to be in front catches hold of a person so badly that the man goes on racing his whole life: "I have to be ahead of everyone." And the crowd is so tremendous, that no matter where you may be, someone is always ahead of you. It hurts you and it saddens your heart.

I used to be the guest of a family in Kolkata. The man owned the most beautiful building in Kolkata, with a beautiful garden. When Kolkata was the capital of India, this house was the Governor General's residence, so this man was very proud of his house. Except for the house, he hardly talked about anything else. I stayed in his house several times. I would say, "I have seen your whole house, I am familiar with every inch of your house by now. Have mercy on me! How long can I listen to this eulogy again and again?"

But when I stayed at his house for the last time, I was very surprised. He was completely quiet – not a word about the house. I said, "Say something about the house! It feels a little odd. You, and sitting so quietly!"

He said, "There will be no talk of the house anymore. Can't you see out at the front? Somebody has built a palace. And until I have built a better, bigger and taller palace than his, there will be no talk of this house. Now, the subject is no longer about the house."

I said, "It is still the same beautiful house. These are still the same beautiful, historical things!" And I said, "He has built a house, but he has not even touched your house. Your house is exactly the same as it was before. Why do you feel so troubled?"

Coincidentally, the person who had built that other house was also familiar with me, and knowing that I was there, he came to see me. He invited me for dinner at his place and of course, along with me, he invited my host too. After inviting us the man left and my host said, "I cannot step inside that house. I would rather that palace caught fire. Even at the cost of my life I will make sure it is destroyed."

I said, "That fellow is a good man. He came to see us. He has invited you."

My host said, "This has nothing to do with being a good man or anything else. He has nasty ways. He wants to find a way to show me the inside of his palace and his belongings. I don't even look at his house! I have put curtains on my car windows. I have raised the boundary walls of my garden. I just want to forget, somehow, that that house even exists. You will have to go there alone. Please forgive me. I will not be able to come with you."

What madness! But every child is being fed the poison of ambition from the time he is still on his mother's breast: "Don't die without achieving something. Prove yourself! Leave your name in history. Make the world remember that you existed."

And you may reach the highest of positions, accumulate all the money in the world, live in great palaces – and then begins the real trouble: "Is this what I have been running after my whole life?"

Those who couldn't manage are writhing; those who have managed are writhing. Those who couldn't attain are writhing because life has turned out to be a defeat; the ego shattered even before it could form. And those who have managed are writhing because it was such a waste of effort and life to attain what they have attained. There is not a single peaceful moment. There is not a single drop of love to be found, not a single note of music. All is emptiness within, a meaninglessness.

The whole of humanity is suffering from one disease and that disease is ambition: "Go on fighting." Don't even worry whether the whys and wherefores of your fight are right or wrong. Who has the time? Time is short and there is no certainty to life. So the means may be right or wrong, but you have to prove that you are something. And the interesting thing is that it is a defeat on both sides. Defeated, you are defeated. Victorious, you are badly defeated.

Naturally everybody appears to be sick, appears to be restless. Inside everybody there are only flames – flames of envy, jealousy – and no peace, no bliss. No poetry is ever born within us, no dance ever arises within us, and then death knocks on the door, and we have got nothing to offer to death except our tears and a defeated life. The long journey of ambition has come to its final moments. Now it is no longer just a slow burning fire – lukewarm. Now it is burning with roaring flames and the whole world is feeling utterly restless. And there is only one way out: that we free man from ambition.

Ambition only makes one run on the periphery and leads man nowhere. These paths on the periphery, that seem to be moving so fast, go nowhere. Keep walking, keep walking…and they never come to an end. Your end comes but these paths remain, just lying there.

These paths don't end; you do.

In the place of ambition, create self-longing: a desire to know yourself, to recognize yourself, to dive within yourself. This alone is the remedy. And the disease is only one – although its names may be many, its forms may be many. The remedy, too, is only one.

All education is futile, all preaching is futile if you are not taught the art of diving within yourself – because that is where the stream of life's juices flows. You are wandering around on the periphery like a beggar and within you is hidden the potential to be an emperor. In this world only those rare people who have looked within themselves have become healthy. All the rest are unhealthy, sick and insane.

I give value to only one thing – call it religion, philosophy, philosophy of life, or whatever name you want to give it – and that is knowing oneself. And that knowing of oneself is not through books, is not through someone else. That knowing of oneself is through oneself. If you cannot go within yourself, where else will you go? If you cannot dive within yourself for a while, what other oceans do you seek to fathom, and where?

If we want mankind to become healthy; if we want the terrorism that is increasing everywhere and becoming more and more explosive and violent to end; if we want the flames of fire to turn into flowers, then there is only one way. That way is called samadhi, enlightenment.

Become natural, become ordinary; live in equanimity, and do not remain unacquainted with the secret that is hidden within you. The moment you become acquainted with it, a great revolution will take place, the revolution which turns dirt into gold, which turns an ordinary man into a buddha, which picks you up from the ground and takes you to the heights of the stars in the sky.

I have moved around the world saying only this one thing, and have been amazed and astonished that people are not ready to hear it. People close their doors, countries close their doors, because what will happen then to their religions, to their religious scriptures?

I know only one scripture. That is you.

Kabir used to say: "He who learns the few letters of prem, love, becomes a wise one."

I say forget about even a few letters. If you can know just one *akshar*, one letter, one eternal secret that is hidden within you, all wisdom, all intelligence is at your feet.

But then the middlemen of the scriptures, of the churches, of the temples – the Hindus, the Mohammedans, the Christians – have become my enemies. There is a network of priests living on your sicknesses, who become angry. Teachers, universities, the pundits of education become angry because their whole educational system is based on nothing but the race of ambition. Politicians become angry because if ambition is sickness, then the politician is the sickest of all people.

What does the desire to be a politician prove? It proves that someone wants to be a president, someone wants to be a prime minister, someone wants to rise above the crowd and become the master of the crowd. Those who are not even their own masters want to be the masters of the whole world. And in the hands of these sick people lies great power – all the power.

Hence, it has been very easy: poison Socrates, hang Jesus on the cross, stop me from entering your countries, try to stop me from speaking, and if necessary, murder me. But as long as I am alive, I will go on saying this to you: that it is necessary to disrupt those vested interests who are exploiting your sickness and who are making business out of your sickness if you want a world that is healthy, peaceful and blissful.

If you want this world to be like a flower garden in bloom – fragrant, colorful, beautiful – then you will have to listen to what I am saying to you. And if you understand it, the matter will be very easy because you won't have to go to anybody, you will only have to go within. You won't have to beg from anybody; you won't have to climb the ladders of any ambition. Rather, you will have to descend into your silences, into your depths – of which you are the master, which are your birthright – quietly, effortlessly, without making any noise.

And if we can succeed even a tiny bit in imparting a taste of peace, in showing even a small glimpse of the eternal nectar to thousands of people on this earth; if even a slight acquaintance with one's own inner hostelry can take place, man can become healthy. It has not been possible up until now, because up until now we have not supported the Socrateses, we have not supported the Mansoors, we have not supported the Sarmads. Until now we have allowed ourselves to remain as toys in the hands of a few wrong people.

Just a little awakening and paradise is yours.

Osho,
What is my path? Please tell me.

The path is neither "mine" nor "thine." What I have just said is the path. And the path is only one, and the path is the same one for all, and the path has been the same throughout all the centuries. It was the same before, it is the same now, and it will be the same tomorrow.

Do not give any name to this path, because it is not Hindu – what has going in got to do with being Hindu? It is not Mohammedan – what has going in got to do with being a Mohammedan? Let it remain nameless, otherwise, fights over names develop in the world. There is great pulling and pushing, a big tug of war, because everyone claims that his path is the right path. And the path is one! If there were even two paths, some comparison would have been possible over who is right and who is wrong.

Going inward is right and going outward is wrong.

So as I said earlier, this is the path – yours and mine – and also of those who are so deeply asleep that they haven't even asked yet what their path is, and who will perhaps slip into their graves while they are still asleep – without ever remembering why they had come and why they are going, why they had lived and what this life was for. This energy that was resounding in their every heartbeat, that was the driving force behind their every breath; this consciousness – who was it?

This is a very strange world. People read geography, people memorize the names of the faraway stars and constellations – and forget themselves.

I had a geography teacher. On the very first day I said to him, "Please say something about yourself."

He began, "What kind of a fellow are you? This is a geography class. In what context are you asking me to say something about myself here?"

I said, "*Your* geography."

He said, "My life has been spent in teaching geography, but no one ever asked me about *my* geography. Geography is about the world, not about the human beings."

I said, "I will start with you. And if you don't know your geography, first learn it. What will come of knowing where Timbuktu is? Even if one can identify where Constantinople is, what will come of that? And whether one dies in Timbuktu or in Constantinople, it's all the same. The point will be: who were you?"

He said, "Look! If you want to learn geography, talk about that, not about strange things."

I said, "I am talking about geography. I want to understand *my* geography, hence *your* geography comes first."

He said to me, "This will not do. Come with me to the principal."

He asked the principal what he was supposed to do. "I have got this young man in my geography class, but either he will be able to learn geography or I will be able to teach geography! Both of us cannot be in the same class at the same time."

The principal said, "I don't understand. What is the matter? What is this fight about?"

The teacher said, "How on earth will you understand it when I myself cannot understand it? If it was about geography, it could have been understood, but this boy is talking of something that no one knows about. He asks me to explain *my* geography."

I said, "Never mind. If you cannot explain it in school, I can come to your home. If you want to explain it in some quiet, solitary place, I will come there. But first I will understand your geography, only then can I proceed further."

The principal said to me, "My dear boy! Choose some other subject. He is our senior teacher and we don't want to lose him. As far as geography is concerned, I know nothing about it because I have never studied the subject. And I don't know what geography you are talking about. Torture someone else and let him go."

I said, "As you wish. The trouble is going to arise in whichever class I go, because what nonsense! Someone is concerned about Genghis Khan, Tamerlane, Nadir Shah or Alexander, and not concerned about himself at all. And what has anyone got to do with that company of fools?"

I dropped geography and took the history class. The teacher was teaching about Alexander the Great.

I said to him, "Are you not even ashamed of saying 'Alexander the Great'? At least, don't spoil the word *great*. Otherwise what will you call Gautam Buddha, what will you call Socrates, what will you call Pythagoras?

"And do you know that at the time of his death Alexander gave his prime minister and top aides his last wishes, and asked them not to make any changes to them? The short message was: 'When you carry my corpse to the cemetery, make sure that my hands hang outside the coffin.' People thought it was a strange wish – hands are never left dangling outside the coffin. This is not the tradition.

"Alexander said, 'Forget the tradition. It is for tradition that I sacrificed and wasted my life.'

"They asked him, 'But why do you want to keep your hands hanging outside the coffin?' They were curious.

"Alexander replied, 'So that the whole world may see that I came into the world empty-handed and I am going empty-handed, and my whole life has been a wastage. I have nothing in my hands. I am dying a beggar.'

"And you are calling this man 'great' who said himself that he is dying a beggar and that his life has been wasted? You are poisoning the minds of all these people, the students who have come to study here, by using the word *great*. You are putting the idea into their minds too that they should become 'great,' that they should become an Alexander."

Neither can one become great by achieving something on the

outside nor can one become wise by knowing something on the outside. The path is only one – mine, thine and everyone's – to know oneself.

Socrates has said, "Know thyself." This covers everything and there remains nothing more than this to be said.

Osho,
Is there no end to this journey?

There is neither any beginning to this journey nor any end. We are part of the endless, the infinite, the eternal. We have always been and we will always be.

It is another matter that the waves seem to be changing, but the ocean remains the same. Forms change, and it seems as if a journey has been completed and another started, but in reality what is, is eternal. Neither is there any beginning nor any end. And what could be more blissful than this: that you are endless, that you are immortal?

The seers of the Upanishads were engaged in only one search: how to move from darkness to light, from the unreal to the real, from death to deathlessness.

If you live in darkness you live in the unreal. And when you live in the unreal you live in death. These three are part of one syllogism, one logic. When you recognize your own inner flame, you will also recognize the truth – simultaneously, at once. And when you have recognized the truth you have also recognized deathlessness – instantly. There won't be even a moment's delay. This is another logic. Now it is up to you.

Under the influence of the first logic, the journeys you have been carrying yourself through until now have been countless – through countless forms, through countless bodies. It is already so late. But still, those who have known have said: "If a person lost in the morning returns home by the evening he is not called 'lost.'"

If you return home even now, you will not be called "lost." However, it is your free choice. If you want to be lost a little while longer, if you want to wander a little more, if you want to start a few more journeys, if you still have some more interest left in getting thrashed, in being beaten, then don't listen to me, don't listen to anybody. Get thrashed, get beaten; live, die; rot in this womb for nine months, in that womb for nine months. And what harm will it do you? When you die, you will be a burden to four other people's shoulders. At least, one doesn't have to carry one's own body. This is one great advantage on your path.

I have heard...

A Jew was about to die. He was old but very rich. His four sons were sitting near his deathbed. The evening had descended, the sun had already sunk and darkness was setting in. Now the sons started to think about the funeral arrangements.

The youngest of them said, "Our father has so much money, and he always wanted to own a Rolls Royce, but never did. Let's hire one and give the old man a ride in one, at least to the cemetery. Never mind that he won't be alive. At least his dead body will have the ride."

Another son said, "You are naive. You are still a child. After all, as he never had a ride in a Rolls Royce during his lifetime, what is the point of riding in one as a corpse? And once the person is dead, what difference does it make whether he rides in a Rolls Royce or in a Toyota? Even a bullock cart will do; it will be all the same. The dead person doesn't notice anything."

The dying father was listening to everything. The second son concluded, "In my opinion, a Toyota would be the perfect thing. The old man is worthy at least of that."

The third son said, "Toyota? You seem to be bent upon unnecessary waste. I have a friend who has a cart, and what a cart! It is a museum piece. If you brought a pregnant woman to the hospital on it, the child would be born already on the way – it gives such jolts! But what difference does that make to a dead man? And it belongs to an acquaintance so it can be arranged very cheaply indeed."

The fourth son said, "I don't want to be involved in all this nonsense. You will have to pay at least something, even for that old cart. Learn something from your father! I am his real son..." this was the eldest son "...I know him better than you all. I have to respect the legacy of my father. The municipal garbage trolley goes to the cemetery every day; it carries the beggars and all who may have died on the road. And when one is dead, what difference does it make if it is our father or a beggar? Just put him against the garbage bin and the municipal trolley will take him away."

At this, the dying father suddenly said, "Where are my shoes?"

The sons said, "Oh! Are you still alive?"

The man said, "I have heard all of your talk. You are all worthless! You don't know anything except how to waste money. All the time wasting money! Bring my shoes. I have still some life left in me. I can walk down to the cemetery myself. I will die right there, at the cemetery. All this trouble and expense for transportation! What if someone recognizes me when you put me out there at the garbage dump...and I die there! Everyone knows me, the whole town knows me. The driver of the municipal garbage trolley must know me. Anyone may recognize me. What will people say? You are neither worried about the disgrace, nor about the expense. You are talking like great aristocrats – Rolls Royce, Toyota, cart! Have your forefathers ever sat in any one of these?"

However, it is your choice. Live, die. Live again and again, die again and again. But one day, some day, you will have to come to the right path. There is no way out. There is no exception. One day you will have to think, "Enough is enough! Now it's time to move from darkness to light. Now I want to travel not from one body to another, but from darkness to light. Now I have to move not from one form to another but from the unreal to the real. And now, no more of entering one house from another. Instead, I want to discard death and embrace deathlessness.

Then, there is no end. Then, the journey is endless. Then, the journey is in the endless. Then, you have become a participant, a partner; you have merged into that which is indestructible.

And, until this happens, know well that the light of understanding has not yet arisen.

CHAPTER 12

TRANSFORMING SEXUAL
ENERGY

Osho,
Poverty continues growing in India because the population
keeps growing and the population keeps growing because of
the poverty. In other words, both are competing with each
other. Given the present conditions, how can the population be
controlled when birth control is only optional here?
Please give some suggestions.

It is not as big a problem as it appears to be. The population does not grow on its own; we are responsible for its growth, and poverty is its natural outcome.

The first things that need to penetrate India's consciousness are that population does not grow on its own, we are responsible for its growth, and poverty does not grow by itself, it is our creation. And for centuries we have been taught to live with wrong ideas. For example, we are told that children are gifts of God and also that the number of children we have is predestined. For centuries, religious teachers have been telling us that to prevent children from being born is to oppose God.

All of this seems to imply just one thing: that God's only work is to go on making people poorer and poorer. And this goes against the very meaning of the word *Ishwar*, God. The very source of the word aishwarya, opulence, is Ishwar. The word *aishwarya*, opulence, is derived from Ishwar, God. So if aishwarya gives rise to poverty, if *Ishwar* helps poverty to grow, then this can only be the creation of the priests, religious teachers, politicians and pundits – all those people who live through the exploitation of the poor.

Unless and until we remove this veil from the Indian psyche – that God has any hand in your poverty... And what kind of a God is it that wants to make you poor? But religious teachers, for example, Jesus, go on telling people, to great acclaim: "Blessed are the poor." This certainly gives the poor some consolation for a short while – just like a man who is drowning in worries may feel some temporary relief from taking opium – but this is not going to be destroy poverty nor the worries. And if poverty really is blessedness, then it should be the preferred choice. How, then, can any question of eradicating it arise? In fact, those who are not poor should also be made poor, because why should they alone miss out on this blessedness?

Mahatma Gandhi calls the poor *daridranarayan* – "the poor are the image of God." All these things may temporarily console the poor but they don't solve the real problem in their lives at all. And these consolers become obstacles to solving the real problem.

I would like all consolations, all pseudo relief and all the deceptions and delusions given to the poor to be taken away from them, and for the poor to be clearly told: "If you are poor, you are responsible for it. And if the population grows, you are growing it. And if it is your wish to remain poor and to take this country into more and more poverty...

"By the end of this century the population of India will be one billion. Half the country will be starving. If this is your wish – that half of India cries out in hunger and dies in front of your eyes – then alright, remain stuck to your old ideas. But we cannot be ready to accept that this is the will of God. And if this were the will of God, and if this is the will of God, then it is absolutely necessary to get rid of such a God!"

Before we are able to persuade the people of India to use birth control, it is necessary to change their mental, philosophical, and religious ideas. Then they will have no difficulty in opting for birth control methods on their own.

I was talking to a Christian missionary. He said, "Any method of birth control is against God."

I said to him, "I would like to ask you one small thing. Your definition of God is that he is omnipotent. And a tiny pill defeats your God! God wants to give birth to a child and a small pill prevents God from doing that. So wouldn't it be better if you stopped worshipping God and worshipped the Pill instead? The Pill is more potent."

It is foolish to be told that God is omnipotent and yet be asked not to oppose his will. On the one hand we are told that not a single leaf moves without God's will and on the other we are asked not to oppose his will. There is a paradox between these two. If not even a leaf moves without his will then we may try birth control in a million ways and yet if he wants to give life to a child he simply can. Our prevention methods won't help. And if our prevention methods do work, it means it was not God who was giving the child. We have been producing children and shifting the responsibility onto God. And as long as we shift responsibility onto others, we cannot bring a revolution into our lives. One has to take the responsibility upon oneself.

As soon as the Indian mind can be educated...which is not difficult. As I see it, Indian people may be illiterate but they are not unintelligent. They may be distant from the modern world, but they have enough intelligence in them to be able to create the most subtle philosophy – about the absolute, godliness, heaven and hell, ultimate liberation – and they can grasp all of it. If this is the case, won't they also be able to understand these small, small things? I don't see why not. I am a total optimist.

What is needed is that in each and every village – the colleges, universities and schools are there, the teachers, professors and students are there – we should make it mandatory that unless and until a student spends two months in the villages, explaining to people about birth control, he won't be able to obtain his academic degree. And unless and until every teacher spends two months of the summer vacation in the villages explaining birth control to people, he will not qualify for any future promotion. There are so many teachers and so many students in India, and so many people who are not teachers and students but who want to be of some help, some service to India. They should all go from village to village and explain to people that there is no opposition to God in birth control.

This is one dimension. And the second dimension is that the government of India should certainly declare that the people who are misleading the masses of India are criminals – the Christian missionaries, Mother Theresa…whoever else is doing it. The pope is to visit soon. Before he arrives, India should understand that these are the people who are misleading the public, saying that the use of any kind of birth control method is irreligious and a great sin. That is their politics, that is not religion. The more orphans Mother Theresa finds, the more the number of Catholics grows. And we are so stupid that we go on heaping more and more awards on women like Mother Theresa without seeing that behind this service to the poor, behind this service to the orphans, there is nothing but the expansion of Christianity.

I haven't seen a single man in the whole of India who is well cultured, well-to-do, and has become a Christian. Those who have become Christians are beggars, orphans and tribal people. And they too have not become Christians because they have understood that Christianity is a superior religion to their own, but rather because Christianity gives them bread, clothes, hospitals and schools.

Whosoever teaches opposition to birth control in India should be punished. At the present time, this is the biggest crime. Such a serious punishment is given to someone who takes another's life – we take the offender's life – and those who are preaching to let the population grow will be responsible for hundreds of millions of deaths. And for these people we have no criminal law, on the contrary, we reward them with more and more degrees, doctorates, and Nobel Prizes.

This double standard has to stop. Every Christian missionary in this country should clearly understand that if he has to live in this country then these nonsense teachings aren't possible. Otherwise they should leave this country right now. Go to your own countries and preach such things there.

It is very interesting that the population in France is stable and all are Christians there. It is very interesting that missionaries from France and Switzerland come to India and explain to people here to let the population grow, because it is "a gift of God." And the *shankarachryas* and the imams dance to the same tunes because they all carry this delusion, that childbirth has some inevitable connection with God. There is no inevitable connection with God whatsoever. Once we can remove this delusion from the Indian psyche – that God has a connection with childbirth – there will be no obstacle whatsoever to Indian people adopting birth control by themselves.

Together with this, I also want to say that so far we have only looked at things from one side – that of birth. So far we haven't considered things from the other side – death. This thinking is incomplete and I want to say the whole thing. Publicize birth-control. Explain to people that now there is no greater crime than giving birth to children, and that you are carrying out this crime against your own children, because it is your children who will starve, it is your children who will suffer as beggars. Your children will suffer hell on earth and you will be responsible for it. If you had wanted to, you could have stopped it. This is one side.

The other side is that if, after seventy-five years of age, anyone wants to choose euthanasia, we should make it legally acceptable. In every hospital there should be a temple-like place where anyone who is over seventy-five and who decides that they have lived fully, have known everything there is to be known, have experienced all there is to be experienced, and that now life is only a burden and they want to vacate their place for a younger person... And it is not that they are committing suicide out of any anger, any defeat or frustration, but rather as the result of reflection and thought. Then they should be provided with all that they may not have had even during their lifetime. They should be given the best facilities: so that they can listen to the most beautiful music, they can meet their friends, their near and dear ones, and they can be given the kind of drug where they slowly pass through the depths of sleep, descending into death. Along with this something like that of a meditation process can be given so that death is not merely death but becomes samadhi, a state of self-realization.

So on the one hand we should stop children from being born, and on the other, for those who are simply dragging themselves around because it is a legal compulsion to live and so they have to live, every one of them should be given their birthright: to leave life. If we start pruning from both these ends, then it is possible that by the end of this century our population will have become balanced. And with the population becoming balanced, there will be no difficulty in destroying poverty.

Osho,
In July when you were in America, you said in the discourses
that no children should be born in India for several years. I said
this to many people after coming back to India. Different people
reacted differently, but most of the women said: "How then to
satisfy the instinct of motherhood that is there in every
woman?" Several said, "A woman cannot be fulfilled until she
becomes a mother." Osho, could you say something about this?

The first thing: How many women in India have attained to fulfillment? Every woman is a mother to one to one and a half dozen children – where is the fulfillment? These children have consumed her whole life; fulfillment is nowhere to be seen.

The second thing: "A woman attains to motherhood by becoming a mother." This is not true. Almost every woman gives birth to children, becomes a mother, but no dignity, no splendor, no luster of motherhood is anywhere to be seen. Hence, my definition is different. In my definition, it is not necessary to become a mother to know motherhood.

All female animals become mothers. In the whole of nature, wherever there is a female, there is a mother. But where is motherhood? Don't take motherhood and mother to be synonymous. It is possible that someone is not a mother and yet experiences motherhood, and it is possible someone is a mother and does not experience motherhood.

Motherhood is an altogether different thing. It is the dignity of love.

I would like women to attain to motherhood. But to have to give birth to children for that attainment is absolutely unnecessary. Yes, to feel every child as your own child is certainly an inevitable necessity for that attainment. It is necessary to let go of jealousy, animosity, envy, to attain to motherhood. And then in our country where there are already so many children without mothers, any woman wanting to give birth to her own child to experience motherhood will never really have it. Where so many children are crying as orphans in search of a mother, to be trapped in the mere idea that the child should be born through your own body? Holding on to such a petty view, no woman can attain to that exalted state of motherhood.

When there are so many children suffering as orphans, there is no need to give birth to a child. Make these children your own. In adopting them, in making them your own, that gap called "mine" and "not mine" will disappear. In making them your own, the petty emotions of jealousy, envy and animosity will disappear. And the bliss that will be attained by raising them, in seeing them grow and blossom, cannot be attained by watching your own children becoming thieves, becoming dishonest, becoming beggars, rotting inside jails.

Motherhood has nothing to do with biology; hence, except for humans, no animal can attain to motherhood. Every female can become a mother but the possibility of motherhood is available only to woman. And that opportunity is available everywhere.

The first thing: motherhood has nothing to do with the physical, biological birth. Rather, it has to do with a spiritual love, a feeling. The moment you make someone your own, as if you have given birth to them yourself... And what is the difference? Who has given birth to a child makes no difference at all.

So there are many opportunities for motherhood. If so many orphans can find mothers, there will remain no need for people like Mother Theresa, who are exploiting these children. And these orphans are being adopted by Catholic families while the women of India are busy experiencing motherhood through giving birth to their own children!

The second thing: it is true that a woman's fulfillment is in her becoming a mother. Hence, when I started initiating people into sannyas, for men there was the traditional word swami for their name, but for women there was none. For thousands of years women have been suppressed so badly, destroyed so badly in India, that they have never been given the opportunity to be initiated into sannyas. So there was no word for them. After great consideration I accepted the word ma, the mother, because it is in motherhood that her fulfillment lies. But this fulfillment of a mother is in the experience of your love becoming so exalted that everyone in this whole world becomes your child – even your husband. And this is how the blessing of the sages of the Upanishads goes as well.

Whenever a couple approached the sages of the Upanishads for a blessing, the sages used to bestow a very unique blessing found nowhere else in any other scripture of the world. The sage would say, "Oh young woman, may you become a mother of ten children and finally may your husband become your eleventh child. Until this happens, understand that life's journey has not been fulfilled." And the day a woman can take, can know, can live with even her own husband as her son, who in the whole world will not then be her child?

Certainly the fulfillment of motherhood is the ultimate glory for a woman. Not through creating a row of children, but through taking your love to such heights that from there every person becomes your own child.

These truths need to be taken to the people, because they are continuing to produce more and more children under grave misconceptions – and they don't even look back to check if there is any truth in these concepts. There are thousands of millions of women, rows upon rows of children, and what motherhood is there? There are thousands of millions of woman, but what fulfillment exists?

People ask me, "You call your female sannyasins 'Ma.' This sounds very strange! Neither do they have children nor are they even married. Even when you give sannyas to a small baby, you call her 'Ma'!" I can understand their amazement. In my vision, even the smallest baby girl is carrying the seed – in the ultimate sense – to enable her to become a mother to the whole world. To address her as "mother" is to give a call to that seed. It is to incite a provocation, it is to throw a challenge to her potential. And the day a mother's love becomes equal for all, and intimate for all – in which there is not any trace of the physical, in which there is not even a far away smell of sexuality – that day a woman attains to fulfillment.

Osho,
If the parents meditate before the woman's pregnancy and
during the pregnancy, what effect does it have on the child?

Certainly the child's life does not begin after its birth. It begins at the very time of conception. It is not only the child's body that is being created in the mother's womb, it is his mind also, his heart also. If the mother is unhappy, anxious, worried, then these wounds will be left on the child as well. And these wounds will be very deep. Even with a whole life's effort the child won't be able to wash them away. If the mother is angry, is quarrelsome, makes a big thing out of every little matter, all of this is going to have an effect on the child. The father's impact on the child is very small, almost nil. It is the mother who creates ninety-nine percent of the child; hence her responsibility is more. The father is only a social institution.

There was a time when there was no father as such, and again there will be a time when there will be no father. But the mother has existed in the past and the mother will also exist in future. The mother is natural, the father is social. The father is only an institution. His function is very ordinary. It can be done by an injection, and it will be done by injection in future, because it can be accomplished in a better way through injection.

In one single ejaculation man releases around a hundred million sperm into the female body, out of which only one succeeds in the race to reach the mother's egg. The one that reaches first enters the egg and then the egg closes. The remaining one hundred million live sperm die within two hours. Their life span is two hours. It is a terrible race and it is a long race. In terms of size, if we accept the height of a man is six feet, then the sperms are so small in comparison that the route to reach the mother's egg becomes two miles long. The competition is terrible on this two mile route. This, I call the beginning of politics. Those who succeed in reaching are not necessarily the best.

It is possible that amongst the one hundred million who were left behind there may have been an Albert Einstein, a Rabindranath Tagore, a Gautam Buddha. No one knows who was left behind, and the one who will be born is accidental – it is possible simply that he was in the front. It is possible that because he was more powerful, he reached first.

But being more powerful does not make one a Rabindranath. Rabindranath himself was the thirteenth child of his parents. It is mere coincidence that Rabindranath could make it in this race. Often it is the case that people like Rabindranath Tagore, people like Gautam Buddha, people like Albert Einstein, are not very interested in running or in any competition. Perhaps we are missing out on the best potential for humanity, which could have easily been chosen. Science is going to accomplish this. If we can choose the best out of one hundred million sperm, why then give the place to even number two or number three?

So the father's role is about to come to an end. But the mother's role is unavoidable from the time of conception.

And this has been my whole teaching – which has been misrepresented with all kinds of distortions – that sex is the starting point of man's life, is everything of man's life. And instead of repressing sex, thought should be given in the direction of how we can make it more beautiful, more elevated; how to take it toward godliness and how to transform it.

Through repression we only give birth to sick people, and meditation is the process of transforming man's sexual energy.

If, in moments of sex, the man and woman are both peaceful, silent, so absorbed in each other that there is no wall between them – as if, in that moment, time has stopped, as if the whole world has been forgotten; where there is neither any thought, nor any concept, but only a bliss, a light into which both have merged.... If the child is born out of such a luminous moment, then we have taught him the greatest lesson on his very first step. We have taught him how one goes from darkness to light. We have given him the first experience of meditation; how everything can be full of silence, peace and bliss.

And if the mother lives through those nine months keeping the child in view – if she doesn't do anything that is against meditation and if she does everything that is conducive to meditation – then certainly in these nine months a buddha can be born. And for those nine months the child will experience love, he will experience peace, he will experience light. If in those nine months he experiences only one thing – the grandeur of his soul – then that child won't be an ordinary child when he is born. That child will be extraordinary. Then we have laid the right foundation stones for his life, and the temple that will rise up from that foundation cannot be any different from it.

That is why whenever any parents come to complain to me about their children, I always tell them: "This may hurt you, but you are responsible. You must have laid a wrong foundation. If today your child is a criminal, if today your child has murdered somebody, then tell me what you were doing in those first nine months when your child was in the womb. What have you done to give him such a foundation that it would not have been possible for him to become a criminal? Perhaps you have never thought about it."

Certainly meditation is useful in every experience of life. And birth is the greatest event of one's life. And in moments of love, meditation is the easiest, the simplest thing, because in moments of love thoughts cease spontaneously, and an absorption surrounds you, a silence surrounds you, a realization arises that we are not separate from existence, we are one with it.

This unique understanding was born in India.

If India has given the world anything that it can claim entirely as its own, it is the science of tantra. And the whole basis of the science of tantra is this one point: how to unite the energy of sex and the energy of meditation.

I have been repeating this my whole life. But people are strange: having eyes they are without eyes, having ears they are without ears, and in between are the interpreters to explain it to them.

Each and every statement of mine has been misinterpreted. I am present and I could have been asked, but no one is concerned with knowing the truth. The only concern people have is that no harm may come to their ideas. It doesn't matter if their ideas lead them into poverty or into crime. It doesn't matter if their ideas degrade them below the level of being human and lead them into animality. All that is okay...just no one should touch their ideas! Their ideas are so fragile that they are almost beyond cure. And the only crime of my life has been that I wanted to help people become free of every idea that in any way degrades them.

This will be the most significant thing: that every couple takes a vow that until and unless they become capable of meditation, they will not give birth to any child. What is the use of giving birth to Genghis Khan and Nadir Shah and Adolf Hitler and Mussolini? If one has to give birth at all, then let it be to someone worth giving birth to: some Buddha, some Mahavira, some Nagarjuna – someone who will refine your intelligence and take you forward. But for that, first of all the parents will have to be ready. And as long as one has not matured into meditation, the person has no right to give birth to children.

My own experience of having worked with thousands and thousands of people is that if the man and woman have both learnt to become orgasmic through meditation, then in the moment of intercourse, only that sperm out of one hundred million which is in tune with their meditation will reach the mother's egg. The reason is that their meditation, their combined energy, will give energy to that sperm. That energy will become its speed and it will leave all the others behind.

To reproduce children without knowing meditation is a waste of life energy.

Osho,
There is a population explosion in the world. I have heard the
saying that when the weight of humanity grows too much on
the earth, nature does not tolerate it. Is there any truth in this?

This is the biggest foolishness of man. He always wants to shift the responsibility of the faults of his own actions onto someone else. For example in this saying, "When the population grows too much, when the weight of humanity grows too much..." it seems as if it has grown by itself, as if we have had no hand in it, as if we were watching it grow from a distance – and then nature will take revenge. In this too we are shifting the revenge onto nature. The reality is that we grow the population, and the growth of the population in itself becomes the revenge.

It is not God that increases the population, nor is it nature. Nor does nature take revenge. We are responsible.

But our sayings are very clever. There is nothing in them except nonsense, because we never include ourselves in them. There are many such sayings: "When the sins of the world grow too much, God will reincarnate." As if the sins grow by themselves. And then, too, we are unable to do anything about it, then, too, God has to reincarnate.

And how many times has God reincarnated? – but the sins have not diminished. It seems that God is also impotent in eradicating sin. No power in the world can eradicate sin, because the ones who give rise to sin are alive – and that is us.

I call when a person accepts his responsibility in its totality the greatest religious act in life: when he accepts that whatsoever he is doing, it is he who is doing it, and whatsoever the outcome may be, it will be his doing. This should penetrate every heart like an arrow. Then, certainly there can be change – because if I myself am doing it, I can stop it. If I myself am responsible for the wrong effects, the ill-effects, then why not cut the thing at its very root?

But these sayings provide us with support so that we can go on sitting back and watching it happen, so that the population can go on increasing: "There is no need to worry, nature itself will take revenge."

Why would nature take revenge? Poor nature goes on being crushed under our weight. There is a limit to everything. For instance, India's population at the time of Gautam Buddha was twenty million. The country was affluent, happy, blissful, and could talk of the higher experiences of life. And it had risen from heights to further heights. The whole world knew us only as one thing: India was "a golden bird."

After Gautam Buddha, our downfall began. And I cannot forgive Buddha and Mahavira: I respect them, I honor them, but I cannot forgive them. Maybe they did it unknowingly, but they have contributed to India's poverty growing because they both taught that religiousness is renunciation of the world. And if people start renouncing the world – if a farmer renounces farming, if a shopkeeper renounces his shop, if sculptors do not sculpt statues – if people start renouncing the world, the world will naturally become poor, because it is we who make the world. The world is dependent on our creativity. And both these people taught only one thing: to renounce everything and become a sannyasin.

And thousands and thousands became sannysins, renouncing everything. The productivity, the creativity that had been taking place through thousands of people stopped. The wives and children of thousands of men became starving orphans. And thousands and thousands of people became a burden on the society, because who will feed them? Who will clothe them? The root cause of the whole slavery, the whole poverty and the whole wretchedness of India is hidden behind a seemingly very lofty idea. Renunciation of the world became a virtue, became sannyas.

When I started giving people sannyas, I changed the whole definition of it: not to renounce the world but to live there in such a way as if you are not in it. My definition of sannyas is completely the opposite of the old sannyas. Nothing is to be renounced and nothing is to be caught hold of either. One has to live as if one were acting in a play: even when he plays the role of Rama, he knows that he is not Rama.

And to live in the world but not to belong to it is the greatest art. To renounce and escape is weakness, is cowardice. And a person who is able to live in the world as if acting in a play, lives untouched. No stains are left on him. And because he does not renounce anything, he contributes something to life before leaving it. He creates. Life is enriched by him because he has no lust, no attachment, no infatuation

179

and no bondage with the world; on the contrary it becomes his blissful play.

There is no need for any poverty and there is no need for any slavery. My sannyasins have become a problem for the religions because their whole concept of sannyas is life-negative and my concept is to become completely saturated with life.

All these sayings are dishonest. Let me repeat one thing. This should remain fixed in our hearts like an arrow. We are responsible for every action and we are responsible for the outcome of every action. Neither can we impose our actions and our outcomes on any God, nor on any nature. Once this becomes clear, all the rubbish of this country's psyche can be washed away. We can give this country a new life, a rebirth. And it is necessary for this country to be given this otherwise it will die. The concepts that it has lived by so far can no longer continue into the future. If India goes on living by these same concepts, by the end of this century it will die. It has lived through much suffering, it has lived in many slaveries, but the last suffering is yet to be lived. And it can be prevented.

And it is a simple matter. All our media, the newspapers, radio, television – whatever media there is for taking views to the public – can broadcast these thoughts. And don't be worried. With my kind of thoughts, there will be many questions coming. I am ready to respond to them. I am talking of not letting a single question go unanswered.

All the media should become a means of education – not only a news broadcasting system for the society, but also a news broadcasting system for a social revolution.

So when you broadcast all these ideas, thousands of questions will come. I am always ready. Whatever questions you find relevant, essential, you can always bring them to me.

CHAPTER 13

THE
LIGHT
OF BUDDHAHOOD

Osho,
Meditation has attained to the heights of Mount Everest in this
country. Unparalleled geniuses like Shiva, Patanjali, Mahavira,
Buddha and Gorakh incarnated here. So why is the attraction
towards meditation diminishing in India?

Just now I was listening to a Ghazal by Mehdi Hassan:

> The shoots have come afresh upon the branches – tell him;
> Neither has he understood nor will he – yet tell him:
> The shoots have come afresh upon the branches

This flow of sannyas…the shoots have come afresh upon the branches.

Meditation has never ever died in this country – sometimes above the ground, sometimes below, the Ganges of meditation has remained flowing constantly, eternally. It is flowing today; it will be flowing tomorrow too.

This is man's only hope, because the day meditation dies, man will also die. In meditation is man's life. You may be aware of it, you may not be aware of it; you may know it, you may not know it, but meditation is your innermost being. That which is hidden within your every breath, that which is hidden within your heartbeat, that which is you, is nothing other than meditation.

But the question is significant.

If this country has given the world anything, if India has made any contribution to the world, it is meditation. Then, whether it is through Patanjali, through Mahavira, through Buddha, through Kabir, through Nanak...the names may change but not the contribution. With different names, through different people, in different voices, we have been giving a single call – one summons to the world – and that is of meditation. Hence this question naturally arises: that after touching the heights of Everest, after recognizing the heights of Gautam Buddha, why then is this disinterest in meditation spreading throughout the collective psyche of India?

On the surface it seems paradoxical, but such is man's psychology. Anything that has already been achieved by someone loses its challenge for the common man. The ego only feels challenged by something which has not yet been achieved, by something which is very difficult to achieve.

Try to understand this. It is subtle.

We have seen Mahavira, we have seen Buddha, we have seen Parshwanatha, we have seen Kabir, Nanak, Farid and thousands of other mystics. One thing has entered the collective unconscious of the masses: that meditation is something which anybody can attain; there is nothing great in attaining it. Farid attained it, Kabir the weaver attained it, Raidas the shoemaker attained it. For the ego, the challenge of meditation has vanished. To achieve money seems difficult; meditation has begun to appear simple. People have begun running after money, after position, after prestige. Challenge is found only in that which is difficult, which has the potential to satisfy the ego. That which is simple, natural and easy...there remains no attraction in it for the ego.

The shining, luminous quality of meditation that was found in so many, took away the challenge of meditation in the common man's mind. And it was felt: "We can attain it – if not today, then tomorrow; if not tomorrow, then in the next life. There is no rush. But who knows if we will come to experience the momentary pleasures of the world tomorrow or not? Today, youth is here, but there is no guarantee that it will also be here tomorrow. If we were to guarantee it one way or another, it seems more likely that it won't be here. It is okay to postpone meditation until tomorrow." This youth, these rising waves of youth, must be satisfied today.

And meditation is attained even by those who have nothing. We have seen the light of meditation with a naked Mahavira, we have seen the luminosity of meditation with the shoe-stitching Raidas. The attraction toward meditation has faded from people's minds. They feel as if it is something that can be had at any time. But wealth, position, status – these countless races for worldly ambition – are not so easy to attain. There is big competition, cutthroat competition. One has to fight for every inch, and only then, somehow, does one become the president of a country of millions and millions of people.

This is the joy of the ego, that "I should be on top of everyone." And the difficulty with meditation is that it says, "The joy of being the last cannot be found when you are sitting on top of everyone. Being last, there is no competition; being last, there is no struggle. No one can push you aside and move ahead of you in meditation because it is not a matter of the outer, it is a matter of the inner. There, you are absolutely alone; there is neither any competition nor any snatching and grabbing."

The ego is not interested in this. The ego is afraid of its death. If meditation flowers, the ego will die. If the flame of meditation lights up, the lamp of the ego will be extinguished. Both things cannot happen simultaneously; they do not coexist. Either it is the ego or it is meditation.

Meditation is within you. The outer world is the realm of the ego and its allurements are many.

What allurement can meditation have?

The ego promises many things, but it never fulfills those promises. It cannot. It is very impotent.

I have heard a story:

A man had been worshipping Shiva and harassing him for a very, very long time. What else is worship if not harassment? – just one tune, just one refrain: "Oh Lord! Give me something so that my life will become a joy! I am asking you only this once, but give me something so that there simply remains no need to ask for anything anymore."

So after constant pestering, tremendous harassment…because this man took no heed whether it was morning, evening or night. Any time he woke up, it could be in the middle of the night, he would be after Shiva. Finally Shiva gave the man a conch shell so he could fulfill his wishes. And Shiva said to him, "The special thing about this conch shell is that from today, whatsoever you will ask it for, it will give it to you. Now, you need not bother yourself anymore: there is no need for worship and prayer. You can leave me in peace! Whatsoever you want, simply ask the conch shell for it. It will provide you with it instantly. Just ask, and the thing will be given."

The man tried it. He asked for a palace to be built and it was instantly done. He asked for a huge pile of gold coins and that was given. He felt blessed beyond measure. Even if Shiva hadn't pleaded with him in such a way, he was bound to forget Shiva. He just forgot all about him: where Shiva had gone, what might have happened to him, what calamities might have befallen him. The man simply couldn't be bothered to worry about all of that. There was only his conch shell and whatsoever he desired….

But then trouble arose. A saint came as a guest to his palace and the saint also had a conch shell. This other conch shell was exactly like his own, except that it was twice as large. And the saint used to keep it very carefully. He did not possess anything else. This big conch shell was the only thing in his bag.

So the man asked the saint, "Why do you keep it under such strict surveillance?"

The saint said, "It is no ordinary conch shell. It is *mahashankh*, the great conch shell. Ask it for one, and it gives you two. Ask it to build one palace and it builds you two. One is out of the question for it – always."

The man became greedy. He said, "This is amazing! I also have a conch shell, but a poor one – a mini-sized one. You have unnecessarily made me a poor, wretched fellow. Now I am a poor man. Let me witness the miracle of your conch shell."

The saint said, "It is next to impossible to witness its miracle. In the deep silence of the night, exactly at midnight when everybody is asleep, is the only time you can ask it for anything. Stay awake tonight and you can hear it for yourself."

Exactly at midnight, the saint asked the conch shell, "Give me a Kohinoor!"

The conch shell said, "Not one. I will give two."

The saint said, "Alright, two; give me two."

The conch shell replied, "Not two, four. Are you aware whom you are talking to? Talk sensibly."

The saint said, "Alright brother, give me four."

The great conch shell said, "Now I will give eight."

The man heard all this and said to himself, "This is great! What kind of a poor conch shell am I holding on to?" He fell flat at the saint's feet: "You are a great saint – a renunciate and a man of austerity. Take this poor man's conch shell and give me your great conch shell."

The saint said, "As you wish. I have always wanted to get rid of it, because this dishonest fellow has harassed me so much! You ask for something, and there is so much talking – sometimes the whole night passes."

Still the man didn't understand what the matter was – that it was only a *mahashankh*, that it only talked, that it never delivered anything at all. It always only doubled the figure: if you said four, it would say eight; if you said eight, it would say sixteen. If you said, "Okay, okay, sixteen," it would say "Thirty-two." No sooner had you uttered a figure than it multiplied it by two. It only remembered a multiplication of two. It did not know anything else.

The saint was gone by the morning. When the man asked the new conch shell for something at an auspicious moment in the night, it announced, "You unworthy man! Why do you ask for one? Take two."

The man said, "Give me two then."

The conch shell said, "I will give four."

"Alright, give me four."

It said, "I will give eight."

The dawn started to approach and the figures were lengthening.

The people from the neighborhood assembled, wondering what was going on. The whole neighborhood was awake to witness the scene: the figure went on increasing but there was no transaction.

Finally, the man asked the shell, "Brother, would you give something as well or will this continue to be mere talking?"

The conch shell said, "I am a *mahashankh*. I know only mathematics. You can try. Whatsoever you ask for, I will double it."

The man said, "I am being killed! Where is that saint?"

The conch shell replied, "That saint has wanted to get rid of me for a long time, but he was in search of the real conch shell. Now he has left with the real thing! You won't find a trace of him, but I can arrange a meeting for you with him."

A conch shell has no feet, yet somehow the man bowed down at its imaginary feet and said, "Please, arrange a meeting with that saint, whatever the cost."

The conch shell replied, "I will arrange your meeting with two saints."

This was the limit. What a hopeless thing he has landed himself with! "I will arrange your meeting with four..." again the same rubbish talk....

Within a couple of days the conch shell drove the man crazy. It would coax the man to ask for something. The man would start looking sideways, because he knew that once you open your mouth this evil shell will have you in its trap. Speak, and you will be in the trap – and then it becomes difficult to drop out of its noose, then it goes on harassing you: "Would you take thirty-two? Would you take sixty-four?" And there is no give and take whatsoever.

The same is the picture with meditation and the ego. The ego is a *mahashankh*, the great conch shell. No matter how much you achieve, it wants more. The numbers go on increasing, the race goes on becoming faster, and man never reaches that place where he can say, "Okay, now here is the destination." The destination always remains a mirage, always the same distance away. There is a lot of journeying, but it reaches nowhere. The hustle and bustle is tremendous. And because the whole world is involved in this hustle and bustle, there is great struggle too – and neither does the mind want to accept that so many people can be wrong.

People rarely take the time to sit down for meditation

Did you pay attention to one word, *buddhu*? It is derived from the word *buddha*. If someone sits down with closed eyes for meditation, people call him "buddhu," the village idiot: "Did you see this *buddhu*? He is trying to become a buddha!" You set out to become a buddha, and you end up only a *buddhu*. "And even if you attain yourself," the ego asks – it is very logical – "even if you attain yourself, what is the big deal in this attainment? You had never lost yourself in the first place. Attainment is about something that is far away. What is there in attaining that which you already are?"

And it sounds logical; it appeals to the intellect. That which is already with me, which is with me since birth, which is my very nature – what the hell is there to attain? It is wasting time! Let us go and attain something that is far away. Let us go to the moon. Let us climb Mount Everest.

What must the taste be of climbing Everest? What taste must Edmund Hillary have had standing on top of Mount Everest?

The story I have heard is...it does not sound believable, but my heart wants to believe it...

When Edmund Hillary arrived with Tensing on the top of Everest he saw that a saint was already there puffing on his chillum. Edmund Hillary hit his head – it had all been for nothing. Before Hillary, some one hundred expedition groups had failed and some had died. Some couldn't even be traced as to what had happened to them, in what snow blizzards they had vanished forever. It was an arduous journey. After tremendous difficulty, Hillary had somehow reached – and this baba saint was there, puffing on his chillum. This was too much!

Sitting down, he looked closely to check if this really was a human being or some ghost, because there wasn't any of the necessary equipment and paraphernalia for reaching Everest next to him – only a metal staff stuck in the ground. A chillum was in his hands and he was in such a trance that his eyes were closed. Hillary thought this must be some great mahatma, some awakened being. Perhaps he had arrived there through the might of some supernatural power of his. Edmund Hillary fell at his feet.

When he fell at his feet, the mahatma was slightly awoken from his trance. He opened his eyes, and looked keenly, "What is the matter?" Then seeing Hillary's watch, he exclaimed, "My boy! How much for that watch? For a long time I have been on the lookout for a good watch. You have come at the right time."

Edmund Hillary replied, "Oh honored one! You can take the watch for free. But tell me, how did you arrive here?"

What that mahatma said – and that is the point I wanted to mention – was: "How did I reach? This is what I wanted to ask you. How did you reach here? As far as I am concerned, people used to call me a buddhu, the village idiot, so I had come here to prove, 'Look! I am the first man to climb Mount Everest. I am creating history. It matters not if I studied history or not, but I have created history.' How did you reach here?"

Edmund Hillary said, "You have spoken my very secret. This is my intention too: to create history, to be the first man! But brother, don't ever tell anybody that you had already planted your staff here and were sitting puffing on your chillum when I arrived."

The mahatma said, "Don't worry! Many like you have come and gone. I go on sitting here, just puffing on my chillum with my staff by my side. And because of this chillum, who remembers who came and who went? Now give me your watch and move along!"

What interest can there be in climbing Mount Everest? Man can endure all the difficulties of climbing Everest, but he is not ready to endure even the slightest trouble when going inside himself. He can go to the moon, taking his life in his hands, and just recently those seven people who were going to the moon died in the middle of their journey, but the idea of going within oneself does not appeal to the ego.

You have asked: "India has touched the heights of meditation, then what happened? What calamity happened? Why did the Indian mind become disinterested in meditation?" – precisely because of having touched those peaks. When so many people have touched the peaks, the Indian ego has lost all desire to go in that direction. Hence today, no other country on this earth has become as materialistic as India has. Although we may be talking endlessly of spirituality, all our spirituality is only babble – the babble of a mahashankh. Our reality is that we are utterly materialistic.

After being in Western countries for five years, I can say now, on the basis of my own experience, that nowhere else on this earth does there exist such a materialistic society as in India. No other people hold on to money with the same force that Indians hold on to it. People spend money; they do not hold on to it. People live money; they do not imprison it. People use money; Indians lock it in their safes. Whether money is confined in the safe or the safe is empty – what difference is there between the two since you will never use it?

I have heard:

A man had two bricks of gold. He had buried them in the backyard of his house and although they were buried, his heart was forever hovering there. A few times each day he would take a walk to the spot, and at night, too, he wouldn't be able to sleep properly.

Many times his wife would say, "What is the matter with you? You are always going out to the backyard and you are always going to the same corner. I will have to get your grave dug there! And what do you go there to look at? I don't see anything."

Now, there was nothing he could say. He was going there to inspect his buried gold bricks – to make sure that no one had unearthed them, that nothing had gone wrong, that there was nothing suspicious going on there.

But wives, after all, are not stones. How long could she go on witnessing this game? One day, the fool went on holiday – and what a holiday! The gold bricks must have been in the back of his mind the whole time. Seeing the opportunity, the wife had the area dug up and confiscated the two gold bricks. She said, "Aha! Now his secret has been discovered."

She took the gold bricks, replaced them with two clay bricks, and had the trench covered over. She made the spot look exactly like it had been before.

Her husband returned. His daily and nightly rounds of the place continued, but now, whenever he went there, the wife would laugh. This puzzled him, because previously whenever he used to go there she would become very angry, call him names and say many outrageous things like: "Is your mind all in one piece?" "Why do you go there?" "Are your ancestors buried there?" Now, she remained completely silent and merely smiled! In fact, she struggled to suppress her laughter and he could not understand what her mysterious secret was.

This went on for a few months.

One day he became suspicious, that this is a bit too much, because by now his wife simply didn't mention that corner at all! He could go there six times, a dozen times a day, could remain sitting there the whole night, and she simply slept on, unworried. So he dug up the spot, found the bricks but...they were not gold. Then he understood the mystery. He came back into the house and asked demanded of his wife, "Where are the bricks?"

His wife replied, "What difference does that make to you? You were never going to use them. You would have only kept them buried. So whether they are of clay or of gold – what difference does that make to you? You just walk round in circles there, so carry on doing that. As far as the gold bricks are concerned, they have already been spent."

Women know how to spend. If you see a husband, does it seem as if he is a beggar, or what? If you see the wife, she appears to have descended directly from royalty. If you see them together, you clearly come to understand that he is becoming a beggar because of her, and she a queen because of him. This is the pact. In this way, both the wheels keep moving together, the bullock cart keeps moving along.

But a great realization happened to that man upon reflecting that he had been circling around bricks of clay. It had been purely a case of belief. He had believed that they were gold. That night he wanted to go to them but he couldn't. There no longer was any point in it.

In this country people keep their money buried in the ground and think they are spiritual – because they do not spend anything. In the West people spend what they earn. And when they spend, it is bound to be visible. When it is visible that triggers Indian jealousy: "These evil ones live only around money. They are materialists. They will rot in hell." And you? Will you walk straight into heaven carrying your filled-up safe with you? No! You are rotting here, you will rot there. They are enjoying it here at least. The future will be seen as it comes. What is the hurry?

India has touched peaks of meditation but that itself has become the cause of its misfortune. Sometimes good fortune becomes misfortune.

In the West, scientists, doctors, surgeons, musicians, writers – so many people – have told me, "Whenever we came to see you in India, the Indian friends who were our contacts, at whose houses we were guests, always made fun of us, laughed at us: 'Why are you running after meditation? What is there in meditation? The whole of the East is coming to the West...and you are one patently mad fellow who is crazy about meditation! And we have witnessed the lofty peaks of meditation in this country – so what? What has come of it? People are starving. Do you also want to starve? So go back home – nothing is lost yet.'"

In the mind of India, in the minds of the greater masses of India, other things have occupied the place of meditation. They are interested in wealth. They are interested in position, in prestige. And in the West today there has arisen a tremendous interest in meditation.

There was only one reason why the American government destroyed the commune that our sannyasins had created in America. And that was because the commune was attracting the American people of intelligence. All the people of genius were feeling a pull toward the commune in one way or another. And the commune started to create a kind of fear in the mind of the American government – that if people started sitting down peacefully and meditating in this way, then what would happen to the Third World War? If passing through meditation, people became full of love, then what would happen to the American empire that is spread all over the world? If the race for position, prestige and wealth disappeared from the hearts of the people, then American might, the American dollar, would disappear into thin air.

A small commune of five thousand people became such a wound to them that "It has to be destroyed at any cost, it has to be demolished from its very foundations. The commune has to be bulldozed and the former desert brought back in its place." Through five years of hard work we had turned the desert into an oasis. To destroy that oasis became their priority.

The first day when I arrived at the commune, there was not a single bird anywhere. It seemed that the birds and animals were wiser than human beings. Slowly, slowly the birds started coming; herds of deer started coming – you may also have seen the deer like I did. But the wisdom that the deer started displaying in the commune was amazing. They would be standing in the middle of the road. You would go on honking your horn and they wouldn't budge. They knew that this is a community of people who will hurt no one. You had to get out of your car, push them aside by hand – only then would they give way.

And because in America there is a ten-day holiday for deer hunting and in those ten days you can kill as many deer as you want, many, many deer from as far away as they could moved to the commune. The commune had enough space: it was one hundred and twenty-six square miles. Thousands of deer came on their own, as if there was some inner message that there was nothing to worry about there. There, no one was even going to throw a pebble at them; there, they would not be shot at.

The commune had not done any harm to America in any way. It had only turned a desert into an oasis. But this, in itself, became the wound, because those who were in the commune had gathered there for meditation. And if meditation were to catch hold of the American genius, and it certainly is going to...

The destruction of the commune makes no difference, because America is in exactly the opposite state that India is in. They have touched the heights of wealth. Now, there is no great attraction to wealth there. So if you look superficially you may see that there is great wealth in America, but no one there has an unhealthy attraction to wealth anymore.

There were sannyasins in the commune who donated ten million dollars, which was their whole wealth. They did not hold a cent back, did not ask, "What if tomorrow...?" The two thousand million dollars that was spent in building the commune was given by the sannyasins. We did not stretch out our hand in front of anybody else. We did not beg from anybody. No one ever insisted on anyone giving two thousand million dollars.

People there had money, and they had also come to the realization that what money can buy is worthless. There is something greater in life which cannot be bought with money. And now the search, the thirst, the longing is for that alone. Meditation is a collective name for all of this. Love is included in it, compassion is included in it.

Meditation is a temple that has many doors. All that which cannot be purchased with money is included in it.

In the West there is an unprecedented attraction to meditation because the West has never touched the peaks of meditation – no Gautam Buddha has been there, no Kabir, no Raidas. The soul of the West is empty. Its hands are full, but its being is desolate. And this situation has created a repulsion around wealth in the West, while in India, a repulsion has occurred around meditation.

The wheel of life is wondrous. There is every fear that the East will become the West and the West will become the East.

In reply to a question asked by the leader of the opposition in the Indian parliament, the minister concerned said, "Osho and any of his sannyasins will not be stopped from coming to India. This rumor that his sannyasins will be stopped from coming to India is false."

I sent some sannyasins to Indian Embassies in different countries. In the embassy in Athens they were asked, "Why do you want to go to India?" The sannyasin who had gone there said, "To meditate." And you will be amazed to know that the reply the ambassador gave her was, "There is no place for meditation and yoga in India now. We do not want that kind of tourist."

I informed the sannyasin to tell the ambassador that she wants a written reply. "Give me what you are saying in writing." But Indian impotence is such that there was no courage to write that either. He said, "I cannot give it to you in writing."

They will not give permission to go and they will also not give anything in writing. I wanted something in writing so that we could prove that what the minister said in the parliament was a lie.

Here, the police are patrolling from morning till night. Four times, five times a day, they are harassing my host: "How many foreigners are staying here?"

If you have no objection to foreigners coming to me – and that's what you say in the parliament – then be honest to some extent! What, then, is the need to send the police here? And what is this fear of yours about foreigners? Even if they are coming to India to learn meditation, your concern should be for their money. Your attention should be on the financial gain you will make. You have nothing to do with meditation – if they are coming, they will only spend some money here before they go back. They will go back only after putting some money in the begging bowls of the Indian beggars.

But no. The reason is that America is pressurizing India not to allow anyone to come here to learn meditation because there is a nervousness in the West. And that nervousness is that if people become interested in meditation, they will lose interest in the futile work that they are being kept engaged in.

The world is in a strange situation. The West has the desire for a journey into meditation and the governments there are making all-out efforts to suppress that desire. Here, the East has touched the sky of meditation – that is our very heritage. We can easily make claim to it but we are denying our heritage. For any world to be as blind as ours is perhaps the height of improbability. And in particular, to stop anyone from coming to me is an utter crime, because neither do I see sannyas as being life-negative nor do I want a meditator to escape to the Himalayas, renouncing family and home.

My effort is so entirely different from the old efforts that perhaps the politicians of India and the politicians of the West are unable to even grasp it.

My effort is that you can go on both the journeys simultaneously – because the two journeys are not antagonistic to one another. Meditation takes you within. And the deeper you go within the more your intelligence is sharpened. And the more your intelligence is sharpened, the more you can go on the journey of success in the outer world. I do not take the inner and outer to be enemies. They are two sides of the same coin.

So, neither is there a need for the Indian government to be afraid of me, nor for the American or European governments to be afraid of me. They should actually be completely unafraid of me. The reality is that if they stop me, they are betraying their own people and their own countries, and are pushing them into the hands of those who are against life. It will bring results contrary to what they are intending. They have no idea of my unique and unparalleled vision of life.

What I am saying is that you can become a temple of godliness while living exactly in the thick of the everyday world. And then the more beautiful and rich the temple can be made – a golden temple, studded with gems and diamonds – the better it will be.

There is no conflict between the inner and the outer for me. Yes, it was true in the past that those interested in going in used to oppose the outer. And those interested in living "out" used to oppose the inner. Gone are those days. Why are you still carrying these dead conditionings? And won't you allow anything new to happen in the world?

My experiment is new. There is no need to connect it with any old experiment. I want every single individual to be affluent in all dimensions, for there to be a paradise within him and also outside him.

Osho,
The other day you said, "I am an anarchist." Please explain this.

...Because I respect the individual, and the individual for me is the ultimate unit. The individual's freedom is the ultimate value of life, and so the less the pressure of guns on him, the less the pressure of rules on him, the less the load of disciplines imposed upon him by others, the better. I want to see man free. And I want man to receive such an education, that along with his freedom, the flowers of responsibility can also bloom in his life.

What is the need for government? The need for a government is because individuals are dishonest, individuals are thieves, individuals are murderers. Just think: the need for government is an insult to you. The bigger the need for government, the bigger the insult to you. Police standing on the streets, lofty court buildings – all this does not speak of your dignity. All this is an indication of one thing: that you are not trustworthy. In order to keep you under control, only guns can be trusted, only swords can be trusted, only violence can be trusted.

I am an anarchist in the sense that I want to see man in his ultimate splendor: where his own consciousness, his own awareness, gives discipline to his life, so that there remains no need for any discipline to come from the outside. This task cannot be accomplished in one day. And perhaps this task will never even be accomplished, but at least we should dream for the highest. It may be a mere dream – and all ideals are dreams – but it is fortunate that there have been dreamers in the world and that they will keep coming, and that wherever we find ourselves today it is because of those dreamers. Whatever little fragrance, whatever little perfume occurs... Sometimes, some flower blooms somewhere, sometimes, some lamp lights up somewhere – all this is by the grace of those who have dreamed. Perhaps it could not be accomplished in their own lifetimes, but the seeds that they have sowed, at some time some shower of rain, some soil, will turn them into flowers.

My understanding is that perhaps the day when a government is not needed at all may never come. But my inner being cannot agree to this. My inner being still hopes that that day will come; that that morning will surely dawn one day.

If the night is dark right now, so what? If the night is long right now, so what? If the dawn hasn't come for a long time, so what? Every night has its dawn, and this night will also have its dawn. It may be far away – it may be too far away – but even the hope that we can provide man with that much awareness that the policeman on the street will become unnecessary, that we can provide man with that much peace that the courts will become unnecessary, that we can provide man with that much understanding that he won't have to trespass on anybody's territory. Then the need for a government will keep diminishing – it should keep diminishing, As man's consciousness grows, the governments will wither away.

And this is to talk of an imaginary day when every individual in the world will be full of the light of buddhahood, and this earth – this whole earth – will be illuminated with the light of humankind, and it will be a festival of lights, Deepawali. On that day, there will no longer be any need for governments; there will no longer be any need for governments anywhere. And there will be no need for politicians either. This is a straightforward matter: if people stop falling sick, there is no longer any need for a doctor.

One morning, as Mulla Nasruddin was going to the market, his physician caught hold of him and said, "This is too much! Four months have passed since I reminded you of my payment. I cured your son, and you have neither paid me my fee nor the cost of the medicines. Am I running a clinic or a charity house?

Nasruddin said, "Do not take this matter too far, because the truth is always bitter."

The doctor said, "My God! Something's gone wrong here: the thief is scolding the police!"

A crowd gathered. After all, it was the marketplace, and in this country no one allows any two persons to have a conversation – and then one over such a juicy matter! Nasruddin shouted aloud, "Brothers, come here! Come here all of you! Listen to all this. I am going to expose the truth."

The doctor said, "What kind of a man are you? I am just asking for my fee. There is no question here of exposing any truth. Do you agree or not that I cured your son? That I gave him medicines and came to see him four times?"

Nasruddin said, "That is right, but who spread the smallpox epidemic amongst the whole school? My son! And who should get commission from the huge earnings you made out of the whole thing? In the true spirit of a gentleman I did not come to your house, and I assumed that you would send the commission money yourself; that you would certainly have had some common sense. My son will be useful in the future too. After all, he is my son. Whenever you say, he will spread epidemics – but please talk in businesslike terms!"

The doctor said, "Business? You mean to say I should pay you some money?"

Nasruddin said, "What do you mean by 'money'? Talk of hard cash in rupees, sir. There are at least five hundred children in the school – and all the hard work my son did to spread the disease! Pay some attention to that! Behave like a human being! Talk of settling the account. How much money have you extracted out of those five hundred children? Come, and bring all the accounts with you.

And if you don't come by tomorrow, remember that I am an old Congress party man. I will go on a hunger strike in front of your house from the day after tomorrow. And the whole village will come to know that this dishonest doctor is robbing a poor man."

The doctor replied, "My good fellow! Come with me, come inside. We will sit down inside the clinic and discuss the matter, and decide whatever needs to be decided. It's alright. If it involves money we will sort it out, but please come inside. Do not talk of all this here in the middle of the crowd. There are also other doctors in the village, and there is such big competition."

If there is sickness in the world, a doctor is needed. China is the only country where there has existed a unique law. And when for the first time you try to understand this law, you will feel amazed. The law was that every person had to be individually affiliated to some physician. And the person would pay a certain amount every month to the physician if in that particular month he did not fall sick. In the month the person fell sick, the physician would not get his fee. On the contrary, the physician would have to arrange for the expenses of the patient's family that month from his own pocket.

It looks a little amazing this way, but it is very correct psychologically. It is the duty of the physician that a person remains healthy – and if he cannot keep him healthy, he is liable to the fine. He can take his fee for keeping the person healthy.

In the whole of the rest of the world it is just the opposite. There, we pay for the sickness. And it is a dangerous thing that the doctor has to live on the sickness of a person. It means we are asking him to carry out a job that is contradictory. The longer a patient remains a patient, the more beneficial it is for the doctor. And his duty is to cure the patient as quickly as possible. Now what kind of a dilemma are you putting the doctor in?

A young man came back from university after his studies. He had become a doctor. He said to his father – the father was also a doctor – "Don't worry anymore. Just take it easy from now on. You have worked hard your whole life. Now I have come back. I will run the clinic."

The father said, "Good. I will give you the chance for three days. I want to see how you manage. For three days I will be on vacation, resting."

After three days the son informed the father, "You will be very pleased to know that I have cured the old millionairess who you could not cure for twenty years, in three days!"

The father hit his head, and he said, "If the profession runs like this, what will happen to your younger brothers? And you will have children – what will happen to them? It is because of that old woman that the cost of your studies could be covered. It is because of that old woman that all our pomp and grandeur exists – the car in the porch, the beautiful house, the gardens, all our children studying in the best schools. You fool! You cured that old woman in three days. This is the beginning of the end of the practice! I will have to come back from tomorrow. You do not qualify as more than a drug dispenser. You will take years still to become a doctor. It is a question of experience. You will slowly learn it all; so far, you have only studied books. You haven't seen life."

And this is true. When a poor man falls sick, he is cured sooner – the same medicines. When a rich man falls sick, it takes a very long time for him to be cured. He simply doesn't seem to be recovering; things seem to keep getting more complicated. Better specialists are needed; more X-rays and other tests by experts are required – the matter just goes on snowballing. But the matter is very clear. If you are wealthy, be careful about falling sick. If you have no wealth, fall sick without a care. A poor man can fall sick any time he wants, no problem. But the wealthy should tread the path of sickness with great caution, with utter caution. It is dangerous.

This is the same situation. Because you are unconscious, unaware, the government is needed. And that is why the politicians are against everything that may fill you with awareness.

What enmity could they have with me? The enmity is that I am talking of all those elements that can fill people with awareness, that can bring people consciousness, that can awaken people's souls and that can give people understanding in the real sense and the courage to live through their own understanding. Then, the government becomes useless, the politicians become useless; there remains no need for them. And they want to be needed. They don't want people to grow in meditation or for enlightenment to spread in their lives.

Just think, I wanted to stay overnight in the airport in England, because my plane had already been flying for twelve hours and according to the law, a pilot doesn't have permission to fly any longer than that. So I wanted to stay for just for six hours – it was already midnight – in the transit lounge at that English airport, where any passenger in transit can stay. But the parliament and the government of England had already decided that I should not be given entry into England. And the surprising thing is that entry into a transit lounge is not entry into a country. But officials and official powers are both blind. I tried hard to explain to the chief of the airport that entering the lounge is not entering England: "It is an international airport. Otherwise, what is the meaning of it being an international airport if it is still England? And there is no other exit from the lounge from which I can enter England. I just have to sleep for six hours. First thing in the morning I will be off on my journey. What is the problem?"

He said, "I have no trouble with that. I myself am in trouble. I am feeling troubled myself about why I am stopping you. But here is the file. There are orders from above that you should be harassed in every possible way. And if you insist on your request to stay here, then you must be kept in the jail, not in the lounge, because 'this man is dangerous.'"

I said, "Look for yourself! I am certainly a dangerous man. I have neither bombs nor guns, and yet I am a dangerous man. But what danger can I create in six hours, just sleeping in this lounge?"

It was written in the file, "This man is dangerous. His presence can destroy the morality of the country, his presence can destroy the religion of the country, his presence can influence the hearts of the youth. This man is too intellectually brilliant, so he should not be given any entry into England."

Is being "intellectually brilliant" a crime? And in my sleep at the airport for six hours, will I do all these things or just have my sleep? Will I be destroying the morality of the country, the religion of the country – the religion that they have managed to establish in two thousand years? Will I destroy all that in six hours, in my sleep?

No, their fears are different, and they are not being disclosed. And what is being disclosed is something altogether different. The fear is that all people have potential. All they need is to be reminded. And the beauty of this potentiality is that you may force it into oblivion for two thousand years and yet it can be revived in a split second.

It is exactly like some forgotten thing that you have not remembered in years and then some occasion arises and you say, "Yes, it is just on the tip of my tongue – somehow I remember it but I can't give it the exact words." And the more you try to remember, the more difficult it seems to become. One feels very uneasy. It is a very strange uneasiness, because you know that you know, and yet you can't recall it. That you know the name, that the name is on the tip of the tongue is also clear. At some level you know the name exactly, but there is something in the way of touching that level – as if some walls have been erected, some other information is blocking the passage, some doors, some windows have shut. You are unable to find the route that reaches to that memory point. And then, feeling too harassed, you drop the idea altogether and you move out into the garden and start watering the plants. And suddenly, watering the rose-bush, you are flooded with the remembrance. With so much effort, it was stuck, and without any effort, it has arrived. When you were trying, you were tense. When you stopped trying, you became relaxed, and the memory had the opportunity to surface.

So in a sense, they are right. The religion that they have established in two thousand years is bogus. The morality that they have handed over to people is a lie – because that morality has never made anybody moral. The number of prisons have gone on increasing, the laws have gone on increasing, the law practitioners have gone on increasing, the courts have gone on increasing. If the morality that they had given people had been authentic, had been successful, then all these things should have been on the decrease. But that has not happened. And hence their fear is right, because I want to remind you of that which is your self-nature and which they have kept covered under who knows how many veils. But the success in raising that self-nature to the surface can be achieved in a moment.

I have my self-remembrance. I can remind you of yourself in my presence. My lamp is lit. Suddenly you too can become aware of: "Whatever has happened to my lamp?" Just a little exploration and what has been imposed on you from the outside can fall away as if it had never been imposed.

I am anarchist because I am individualist. The individual has the soul and in the soul is the whole truth of life, the whole nectar of life. And I nourish only one wish, only one longing: that there should arise so much awareness in man that there remains no need for any government, any law or any discipline to be imposed on him from the outside. Far, far beyond the horizon, perhaps, one day this phenomenon will be actualized. But we can at least dream of it. At least there are no fetters on dreams. And a good dream is a million times better than an ugly reality.

Osho,
Problems of crime, punishment and guilt vary with differences
of place and time. But in one form or another they always follow
man everywhere. Would you please throw some light on this?

It is true that the concepts of crime, evil and of being a criminal have changed over the centuries. But in one form or another, in newer and newer forms, the feeling of guilt has basically followed man as a shadow. It is your own shadow and until you become filled with light within yourself there is no way for this shadow to disperse.

Look at it this way: Yudhishthira in the Mahabharata is called *dharmaraj*, "the king of religion." It was a different world then, a different air. Yudhishthira could be a gambler and at the same time "the king of religion" – and he was no ordinary gambler. He lost everything. And when he lost everything he possessed, he wagered his wife. This proves that he had no other feelings for women except for their being objects – they too were things. He wagered the house, the palace, and in the same way he wagered his woman. She too was a possession, a thing. And yet no one in the whole history of India raises any question about why we go on calling this man "the king of religion." And if these are the ways of the king of religion, what, then, will be the ways of the king of irreligion?

But at that time, in those days, gambling was the same as playing cricket or tennis is today. There was no problem anywhere about gambling; there was nothing bad in gambling. It is in repetition of that old memory that the Hindus gamble a little bit on the night of Deepawali, their festival of lights. If not the whole year around, let it be at least one night; if not in a big way, let it be at least a little bit – that you wager ten or twenty rupees. But at least in this way you remain connected with your ancestors, at least you maintain the pride of your tradition. You go on reminding yourself that you are also the descendants of Yudhishthira: "If a situation arises we can also wager our wives." We don't – that is a different matter – because now the women have become dangerous. They, on the contrary, can wager us! The times have changed, but the intentions have not changed in the least.

But the one basic thing that comes across from all kinds of beliefs is that man is unconscious. It didn't even cross Yudhishthira's mind that what he is doing is unconscious and to wager a woman is to insult her. To downgrade her from the level of a human being and to take her to the level of an object can never be forgiven.

The same thing can be found in thousands of other examples. Even today, you are doing many things that seem alright to you, but tomorrow's people will declare you a criminal for those same things.

This story will continue until we bring the maximum number of people into the state of awareness.

The only meaning of awareness is that I do not do a single thing that may take away someone's rights and that may transgress the boundaries of anyone's individuality; that I do not do any act that I may have to hide from others; that I do not do a single act for which I may ever have to repent.

All these points remain present in front of an aware and alert person on their own. Filtering through them, the actions of his life become free of crime, become free of the shadow of crime.

Okay?

CHAPTER 14

THE ETERNAL PILGRIMAGE

*Osho,
What is this dream of yours which you have been working so
hard to realize for the past twenty-five, thirty years, ignoring
all kinds of hindrances and obstacles?*

The dream is one. It is not mine, it is centuries old. Let us call it
eternal. This part of the earth began dreaming this dream from the
very dawn of human consciousness. How many flowers are strung in
this garland? How many Gautam Buddhas, how many Mahaviras,
how many Kabirs, how many Nanaks, have sacrificed their lives for
this dream? How am I to call it *my* dream? This dream belongs to man
himself, this dream belongs to man's inner being. We have given this
dream a name: we call this dream "India."

India is not a piece of land, it is not a political entity, not a chapter
of historical facts. It is not the mad race for money, power and status.
India is a longing, a thirst for the attainment of truth – the truth that
resides in our every heartbeat, the truth that is sleeping in the very
layers of our consciousness. It is that which although ours has been
forgotten. That remembrance, that reaffirmation is India.

"*Amritasya putraah* – Oh sons and daughters of the eternal!" Only
those who have heard this call are the true citizens of India. No one can
be a citizen simply by being born in India.

Wherever one is born on earth – in any country, in any century,
in the past or in the future – if his search is a search of the inner, he belongs to India.

For me, India and spirituality are synonymous, hence the true sons and daughters of India can found in every nook and corner of the earth. And as far as those who are born in geographical India merely by chance are concerned, until they are mad after the search for immortality, they have no right to be called "the citizens of India."

India is an eternal pilgrimage, a timeless path that is stretched from eternity to eternity.

That's why we have never written history in India. Is history something to be written? History is the name given to ordinary, insignificant, day-to-day happenings: those happenings that arise like a storm today and of which there is not a trace to be found tomorrow. History is merely a passing dust storm.

No, India has never written its history. India has only dedicated itself to the eternal – like the *chakor* bird incessantly watching the moon without a blink of the eye.

I, too, am just another traveler on that eternal pilgrimage. And I have only wished to remind those who have forgotten it, I have only wished to awaken those who have fallen asleep, so that India may regain its inner dignity and pride. The destiny of the whole of mankind is connected with the destiny of India. It is not a question of just one country.

If India disappears into darkness then man has no future. And if we again give India its wings, if we again give India its sky, if we can again fill India's vision with the longing to fly toward the stars, then we will have saved not only those who already have a thirst for the eternal, but also those who are sleeping today but will wake up tomorrow, who are lost today but will find their way home tomorrow.

The fate of India is the destiny of mankind. The way we have polished man's consciousness, the lamps we have lit within him, the flowers we have encouraged to bloom in him, the fragrance we have cultivated within him – nowhere else in the world has anyone accomplished this. This has been a continuous discipline, a continuous yoga, a continuous meditation, over some ten thousand years. We have lost everything else for this, we have sacrificed everything for this, but we have kept the lamp of consciousness burning even in the darkest nights of man. No matter how dim the flame may have become, the lamp still burns.

I have dreamed that that lamp of consciousness can again attain to its brightest. And why should it burn within only one person? Why shouldn't every man become a pillar of light?

In no other language of the world is there a word like *manushya* for man. The meaning of the word for man in Arabic and the languages born out of Arabic, in Hebrew and the languages born out of Hebrew, is "an effigy of mud." *Aadmi* means "an effigy of mud"; *man* means "an effigy of mud." Only in the word *manushya* is there the recognition that you are not an effigy of mud. You are consciousness; your nature is immortality. Within you is the ultimate flame of life. The lamp can be made of mud but the flame cannot. This body might be made of mud, but the one who is awake within it, is conscious within it, is not. When the whole world became busy in the pursuit of mud, a handful of people remained absorbed in the search for this flame.

You ask me what my dream is.

The same that all the buddhas have always had: to remind man of that which has been forgotten, to awaken that which is asleep – because unless and until man understands that eternal life is his right, that godliness is his birthright, man is not whole. He remains incomplete and crippled.

From the moment I became aware – each moment, every hour – there has been only one effort, there has been only one endeavor. Day and night, only one attempt: that somehow I may remind you of your forgotten treasure – so that the declaration of "*ana'l haq*, I am the truth" arises from within you too; so that you too can proclaim "*aham brahmasmi*, I am godliness."

God has been talked of in each and every corner of the world, but he has always remained far away – very far away, beyond the skies. Only in India have we enthroned godliness within man himself. Only in India have we recognized the potential in man, the beauty and dignity of man becoming a temple by enthroning the divine within man himself.

How every person can become a temple, how each moment of every person's life can become prayerfulness – this you can call my dream.

Osho,
Your vision of bringing paradise to earth took you to America
and there you succeeded in realizing the whole of humanity's
centuries-old utopian dream. Would you please tell the Indian
people of the achievements of Rajneeshpuram, the American
commune?

It was necessary for me to leave India in order to remind India of India. That which is too close can be easily forgotten. Nobody listens to one's own. Who cares to seek out that which is already there within the house itself?

For some twenty years I traveled to every corner of India and all I received were wounds to my heart. Those whom I tried to awaken were in a deep sleep. And nobody likes his sleep to be disrupted, nobody likes his dreams to be disturbed. Stones were thrown at me, attempts were made on my life. But all this was acceptable to me and I understood that this was inevitable, and I was not disturbed with any of it.

But one thing certainly made me unhappy and that one thing is not concerned with those who pelted stones or threw knives at me. It concerns those who cheered upon hearing me speak. Those wounds are still fresh; they simply refuse to heal. Those people were not cheering for me – that what I was saying was the truth – they were cheering for me because what I was saying was satisfying their egos. They were not ready to bring what I was saying into their lives. They were only clapping and using what I was saying as an entertainment, they were being amused by it. My words became a cover-up for their own wretchedness, their own inferiority, their poverty and their slavery. That's why I had to leave, so that perhaps a call given from afar might be heard by them, and that perhaps in faraway America I could experiment and create a small India.

And I chose America because the very heights of consciousness that India had attained were attained at a time when it was affluent. They had been attained in times when the whole world called India a golden bird. Those heights were not of a helpless, poor, beggarly and enslaved India; for when there is not even stale bread to eat, it is not possible to long for a flight toward the stars and to open one's wings to the sky.

These circumstances were ripe in America. People there had reached the same height of affluence as India once had, and had also discovered what we had discovered at the height of our affluence: that wealth can buy everything but not love, not godliness; that wealth can buy everything but not bliss, not the taste of immortality; that wealth can buy everything but not meditation, peace, or silence.

Only upon attaining wealth does man come to realize that there is nothing poorer than being a wealthy man. In spite of all the material possessions one is utterly empty inside. And an emptiness, a meaninglessness, a deep anguish, that "I have everything and yet I have nothing," follows. America is in this same hour. America needs someone to tell it that there is a world beyond wealth, a world which only a wealthy person can attain – because to attain that world the only ladder can be wealth. It is not attained by wealth but by walking beyond it.

That's why I had chosen America. And within five years, within a very small span of time, this dream was actualized. A desert...it was a big desert, one hundred and twenty-six square miles, where not a flower had ever bloomed. The day I arrived in that desert there was not a single bird there. With five thousand sannyasins, everyone working twelve or fourteen hours a day, within five years we transformed that desert into an oasis. Whatsoever one had – if money then money, if physical strength then the body – everything was gambled. The desert was revitalized. It became an oasis.

Birds came from far, far away. Wild animals came. Thousands of deer came to the transformed desert. We built houses for five thousand sannyasins with our own hands. We did not take support from anyone in America. We built roads, we built lakes. We invited swans: when the lakes were created, swans came. As we created the gardens, the deer came – three hundred peacocks just in my garden! With the onset of the rains three hundred peacocks would start dancing...the colors of the whole world, the celebration of the whole world!

Five thousand sannyasins would eat from one kitchen...

Because my whole understanding is that the time of the small family is over now. Now we need bigger families for man. We need communes.

Five thousand sannyasins would sit down to eat, and someone would start playing and singing on the guitar, and someone would start dancing. And in the festival days, some twenty thousand sannyasins from around the world would come. For them we had created tent accommodation with our own hands – and a kind of tent that had never been built before. Those tents could be used in rain, in snow, in summer, in winter – in all the seasons. Air-conditioning and heating could be installed in them as needed. All the houses for the five thousand sannyasins were centrally air-conditioned.

And all other possible amenities for the comfort of the five thousand sannyasins were there: there were five hundred cars for five thousand sannyasins, there were five airplanes, there were one hundred buses, our own hospital, our own doctors, our own nurses. There was a school, our own teachers, separate residential facilities for the children – the children had their own separate world.

In the morning the work would begin with meditation. After meditation, either people would all sit with me in a silent satsang for an hour, or if I was talking they would listen to me. And then came the work for the whole day, and celebrations again in the evening.

People would sing and dance until late into the night. It was probably the first time ever that five thousand people lived together for five years and no one ever fought with anybody, no theft happened. Neither was there any worries in people's lives nor any question of security for the future, because with five thousand companions and nearly one million of our sannyasins around the globe, one felt that "they will be with me through my joys and my sorrows."

America couldn't tolerate the creation of a world family. And when I say America couldn't tolerate it, I mean the American politicians, the American government couldn't tolerate it. As far as the American public went, they were very impressed. They simply couldn't believe that in this desert where nothing had ever grown, agriculture and farming was happening, fruits and flowers were being produced. We were producing everything for our own needs from that desert: grain, vegetables, fruits and flowers; our own dairy, our own produce of milk, butter, purified butter – everything that was needed by us.

And with this experiment I had included a new thing because our sannyasins are vegetarians and vegetarianism is not a complete diet – there is some deficiency in it, a dangerous deficiency. It lacks the proteins that are needed to maintain the brain. That is why so far no vegetarian has ever received a Nobel Prize. To remove this deficiency, we had thousands of hens at our chicken farm and when chickens lay eggs without coming in contact with a rooster, that egg is unfertilized. It has no life in it. It cannot produce a baby hen or a rooster, but it contains all the proteins that are lacking in vegetarian food. Including unfertilized eggs in the vegetarian meals of the sannyasins was a unique experiment which today or tomorrow the vegetarians of the whole world will need to adopt, otherwise, they will go on lagging behind intellectually.

People from far away places in America started coming to see the commune and the American politicians started feeling uncomfortable. The politicians began to be questioned: "If strangers coming from outside America can turn a desert into a paradise, then how come there are millions of beggars in America who have neither a home nor clothes nor food to eat? They live on the streets." And because I invited two hundred of those street people and included them in our commune, the American politicians got an even bigger shock: the beggars that they could not even give food to had been given the dignity of being human beings. There was no discrimination toward them. They received the same honor, the same respect that should be given to every human being. They themselves couldn't believe it. Some of those street people came and told me: "We cannot believe it because for our whole lives we have been kicked around like dogs. We had forgotten the very idea that we are human beings."

Journalists, TV and radio people from all over America started flooding into the commune. The whole of America became curious about what this revolutionary phenomenon was that was happening. No currency was used in the commune, no transactions in bills or coins. This is why I can say that that commune, Rajneeshpuram, was the first ever truly communist system in history – where no one was rich, no one was poor. You could have millions of dollars, but what difference would that make? Those dollars couldn't be used inside the commune. In the commune the needs of everyone were taken care of – what ever one needed was, one could take – but there was no private buying or selling.

The American politicians faced double trouble. One was that there came into being the purest form of communism, which did not even exist in Soviet Russia. The second was that, based simply on labor and intelligence, a desert had been transformed into an oasis, And it is possible to create a society where no one is unhappy, no one is mad, no one commits suicide; where there is no murder, no stealing, no crime, no fighting; where there are no troubles between Hindu and Mohammedan, Christian and Jews; where there are people from all races, all religions, where there are blacks and whites; where there are people from almost every country, where no one feels any superiority or inferiority to anyone else. Such equality, such communism... One thing settled deep in the minds of the American politicians: that the existence of this commune is not free of danger for them.

And this point recently suddenly slipped out of the mouth of America's attorney general, while fielding questions in a press conference. He was asked: "Why didn't you sentence Osho to prison?"

They had framed me with one hundred and thirty-six crimes. A person charged with one hundred and thirty-six crimes should receive punishment – at least one thousand years of jail, minimum. One would have to reincarnate ten or twelve times to complete the sentence.

The truth slipped out of the mouth of the attorney general, America's top legal official. And this was the man who had led the case against me in the court, saying that I had committed one hundred and thirty-six crimes!

He said three things in the press conference. One: "Our first priority was to destroy the commune." Why, one may ask – what harm had the commune done to anyone? The commune had nothing to do with America. The nearest American town to the commune was twenty miles away. We had such a vast amount of land and no one had the time to go out anywhere, nor the need. To destroy the commune was the first basic aim.

Number two: He said, "Osho could not have been sentenced to imprisonment because he had not committed any crime and we have no evidence against him for any crime."

Man can be hypocritical beyond measure. This is the same man who stood in the court with the charge sheet of one hundred and thirty-six crimes against me, and the same man is also ready to say that neither has he any evidence for any crime nor has any crime taken place.

And the third point is even more noteworthy: "We did not want to turn Osho into a martyr by keeping him imprisoned, because that would have given his religion a very solid base around the world."

The commune was destroyed absolutely illegally. I was arrested absolutely illegally – without any arrest warrant – because they had no reason for the arrest. After the arrest, I was not allowed to contact my attorney – which is everybody's right. The first thing any attorney would have demanded on arrival is to see the arrest warrant and to know the basis for the arrest.

I was arrested at the point of twelve loaded guns. There was no reason for any arrest, only twelve loaded guns! And I was produced in the court. This same attorney general was unable to prove anything, and he accepted this in the court after three days of continuous argument.

Five other sannyasins were arrested along with me. All five were released on bail, but the attorney general insisted that I could not be granted bail. And he himself accepted in the court that he was unable to prove a reason why I should not be granted bail, "Yet I request the judge, on behalf of the American government, that bail is not granted." And the judge did not grant bail.

Even the jailer who brought me back to the jail was puzzled, because he could not conceive that I would have to be taken back to jail. He had brought all my clothes and my other possessions to the court with him, thinking that I am sure to receive bail. These people had neither an arrest warrant nor any reason for the arrest, so there was no reason for the bail not to be granted.

The jailer said to me, "I am puzzled and bewildered. I have never seen a case like this in my whole life. Firstly, the arrest is wrong. The arrest has no substance to it. The government attorney could not produce any evidence and he has even accepted this fact – but the insistence from the government is that this man should not be granted bail." And the jailer told me that the cause behind not granting bail is that the magistrate who was a woman, had been informed that in order to be promoted to the post of federal judge she must not allow me bail, and if she did, she would remain a district judge for the rest of her career; she would never become a federal judge. And certainly she became a federal judge within three days.

Bribing the law and that too being done by governments!

And the place where I was arrested – North Carolina – was only a six hour flight from Oregon. We were ready to provide our own plane to bring us to Oregon where the actual judgment was to take place – in our own plane flown by their pilots, under the supervision of police officers. But no, I could only be taken in a government plane.

And you will be amazed to know that the government plane took twelve days to complete a journey of six hours. This is why it was necessary to be taken in the government plane, because the government plane would break the journey at every airport it landed at. Six jails in twelve days – without any reason. They couldn't do too much to me because somehow the attention of the whole world was on this matter. Still, they tried in every possible way to harm me.

They knew that I had a back problem – it hurts and doctors are unable to treat it. Except for surgery there seems no other way to treat it, and a cure is not guaranteed even with surgery. On the contrary, it can even get worse, so they don't even advise me to opt for the surgery.

The night they arrested me, they kept me waiting the whole night on a steel bench – handcuffs on the hands, fetters on the legs, a chain on the waist, and another chain from the handcuffs to the chain on my waist so that I am unable to even move my hands. Each time, in every jail, that chain was tied to my waist at exactly the same spot where I have the back problem. And I was given the same kind of steel bench everywhere so that they could worsen my back problem as much as possible.

Each time a marshal handed me over to the next jailer I was sitting in the car and he would whisper to the next jailer, "Be very careful with anything you do, because this man is of international fame and the eyes of the whole world are focused upon him. One small mistake will put a black mark against the whole of American democracy, so whatsoever is done should be done discreetly."

In the second jail I was asked to sign in under a false name, not my own name. I said, "This is a little strange! An officer of the law is asking me to sign in under a false name: David Washington! And I am being told that here I will be called by the name 'David Washington'!"

When I refused, saying that I was not ready to do any illegal act, I was threatened with having to wait on a steel bench the whole night. I told them, "Later on you will be sorry for all this because for how long can such things go on? The day I am released from jail the whole world will come to know of all this wrongdoing. And on what basis do you want me to be called 'David Washington'? Even a dim-witted man can understand what it means: that even if you kill me, there will be no way to trace where I disappeared to because my name won't be in your files. And no one will even imagine that I could be this man with the name 'David Washington.' How would anyone think of that?"

So I said, "If you are so keen, write the name 'David Washington' yourself. You fill in the form; I will only make the signature." The jailer also wanted to leave. It was already midnight. Until how late could he sit down and wait? He was in difficulty because he would have to sit with me. So he filled in the form, but he did not realize that by doing so he was making a mistake: the handwriting would be his, and I would make the signature of my own name.

When I made my signature he was puzzled and he said, "What is it this that you have written?"

I said, "It must be 'David Washington.'"

"But in what language?" he asked.

I said, "I will write only in my own language. Nothing was decided about the language." And I said to him, "Tomorrow morning this will be on the news on all the TV channels, in the newspapers and on the radio, that now my name has become David Washington."

He said, "You are threatening me. How is this possible? There is no one else here other than the two of us."

I said, "Look out for it tomorrow morning…"

A young girl who was involved in some crime had also been brought to the jail premises with me in the same car. She had traveled with me in the same airplane. She may have read my books, she may have heard my talks on the TV. She said to me, "If I can be of any service to you…"

I said to her, "Just keep one thing in mind: any conversation that transpires between me and the jailer in the jail…"

The next morning she was going to be released and to leave.

"…the first thing you must do as you go out – and you will meet reporters and journalists right at the entrance as you come out – is to tell them of any conversation you may have heard in here."

And that girl did inform the journalists of everything in exact detail at six o'clock in the morning. The news went all over America on the seven o'clock news bulletin. In utter confusion and desperation, they took me out of that jail at once, because it became very difficult for them to keep me there for a single minute more.

In every jail they tried to hurt me in some way or another. In one jail they forced me to stay in the same cell with a person with whom no one had been kept for the past six months. That man was dying from a very contagious disease, herpes. Anyone in the vicinity was certain to catch the disease. For six months that man had been living in that cell in isolation and since then no one else had been kept in the cell, just to avoid catching the disease. But the doctor was present, the jailer was present, and no one objected in my case. They put me in that room…the man was close to dying, the next day he did die.

That man said to me, "I cannot speak much English…"

The man was from Cuba.

"…but I want to say to you that my sympathies are with you. I am dying anyway, but I don't want you to die from this disease. The effort of all these people is for you to somehow catch this disease. So please, don't move away from the door. Remain standing at the door and keep knocking even if you have to do it the whole night. Do not enter the room. Stay at the door until those people open it.

I had to knock for an hour, and then the jailer came and the doctor came. I asked them, "Aren't you ashamed of putting me here when for the past six months you have not put anyone in this room, when I am not even a criminal? And tomorrow how will you answer the newspapers, the television reporters and the world? This man is more human than you are, and you are a doctor. You should commit suicide. You have taken the oath of medical ethics to save lives and you have remained standing there quietly. What has happened to your oath?"

I was taken to another room immediately. They had no answer at all, but they made every attempt for twelve days continuously that somehow I should be indirectly harmed, that somehow I should be harassed, that somehow I should be given trouble. But those poor fellows couldn't manage anything. I feel sorry for them.

One thing became very clear to me. Nowhere in the world is there a democracy that can really be called democracy. There used to be a respect in my heart for the democracy of America, but what I saw there and what I experienced there before my return to India is that there is no democracy to be found. And Ronald Reagan is a number one Hitler – actually poor Hitler has become number two now!

Osho,
Why are misleading descriptions like "the sex guru," "the guru of the rich" etcetera associated with your name? Is there some conspiracy to keep you surrounded by disinformation?

The conspiracy is big. It should be called international.

If a lie is repeated again and again, it starts to appear as truth. At least four hundred books are published in my name. I have not written a single book; whatever I speak becomes a book. In those four hundred books there is one book titled *Sambhog Se Samadhi Ki Aur.* These are five talks given in Mumbai. Whosoever reads that book would understand that it is not about sex. It is about how to transcend sex. The same book is translated into English as *From Sex to Superconsciousness.* The basic theme of that book is how a person can slowly, slowly – from sex, through the means of meditation – touch the highest peaks of consciousness.

But neither do people read the book nor experiment with the things written in it. Just one word catches their minds. And because the word sex has been used, the journalists, the politicians, the religious leaders – all the people with vested interests whom I am hitting and who are at their wits' end to find any answer to my statements – have caught hold of that one word. And when all the religious leaders, all the political leaders… And all the newspapers are in their hands: they are either in the hands of the religious leaders or in the hands of the politicians or the rich, and they have kept publicizing it throughout the whole world that I am a "sex guru."

The reality is that there is no other person present on earth at this time who teaches you how to go beyond sex.

And the same goes for the statement that I am the "guru of the rich." I have reiterated the point again and again that only those who have wealth are able to see the futility of it; that to know the futility of money, it is first necessary to have some. All the twenty-four tirthankaras of the Jainas were the sons of kings. Buddha was the son of a king. Rama and Krishna were all sons of kings. Have you ever seen the son of a beggar becoming a tirthankara? Have you ever seen the son of a beggar becoming an avatara? The beggar has no time. Before he can call wealth futile, at least he should have wealth. He should have the experience of wealth.

So, because I had said that the emergence of religiousness in the real sense can only take place in the rich and affluent countries, and in India religiousness had emerged only when the country was affluent… What has India got today? Poverty, hunger, disease. All these things can only make you ask for bread. If you go to a hungry man offering to teach him meditation, you will feel ashamed of yourself.

I want this country to be rich. I want there to be no one who is poor in the world, no one who is hungry in the world. And why do I want that? – because if there is affluence throughout the whole world then we can increase the thirst for spirituality a thousandfold. We can spread it like wildfire.

If someone concludes that I am the "guru of the rich," and if the person has the means to publicize it, he can do so easily. My trouble is that I am alone and I am fighting the whole world alone. I haven't even the time to look at all the newspapers that publish things about me in so many different languages.

For instance, just the day before yesterday an Israeli newspaper published the news that I am planning to come to Israel and upon arriving there I am going to declare myself initiated into the Jewish religion. And once initiated into the Jewish religion, I will declare that I am a reincarnation of Moses, the founder of Judaism.

Now what shall I say to these people? And what is the point of even saying anything? And to how many people shall I say it? What goes on being published in all these newspapers all over the world… For seven years I have not read anything. I simply stopped reading because what is the point of reading meaningless rubbish? For seven years I have read no books or newspapers. If something very important happens, my sannyasins bring me the news.

So to spread as many lies about me as possible is very easy, because I don't even come to know what lies are being spread about me. And because I don't counter them, people simply accept them, that they must be true. Otherwise, I would have countered them.

The masses want anything that is sensational and exciting, and the newspapers are always ready to publish just that. Of course, because the powerful will harass them, they are afraid to publish anything against those who have power. If someone is in a high position in politics, not even true things can be published about him. I have no power. I cannot harm anyone in any way. As many lies as one wants can be published about me.

But lies have no life in them, and slowly, slowly it has become clear to people all over the world that there is certainly some conspiracy going on against me.

Just a week ago, the wife of one of my sannyasins, Vimalkirti, was present here. Vimalkirti is the grandson of Germany's last king. He was my sannyasin and so is his wife. He died as a sannyasin. His father, his mother, his brother were all here at the time of his death. The doctors had said on the very first day, "There is no hope for his survival because a vein in his brain has broken..."

And this disease is hereditary. His grandfather had died in this same way; just two months ago his uncle died in the same way.

"He has been in a coma since the vein ruptured and we are keeping him alive through an artificial respirator – but it is an exercise in futility."

After five days the doctors said, "It is wasting our time for nothing. There is just no way to bring this man back. Everything in his brain is dead."

I asked them to at least let his parents arrive.

After the arrival of his parents, they removed the artificial lifeline and he died. He had died seven days ago; we were just waiting for his parents to arrive. A newspaper in Europe published the news that I had had him killed; that I asked for the artificial lifeline to be removed. His wife was present throughout, his daughter was present throughout. At the time of his artificial lifeline being removed, his wife and his daughter were both present in the hospital.

His wife was here recently and she said to me, "You will be amazed to know that the Queen of Greece was a disciple of one of the *shankar-acharyas*. One of the sons of the Queen of Greece, Prince Philip, is the Duke of Edinburgh, the husband of Queen Elizabeth. One daughter is Vimalkirti's mother, the wife of the uncrowned King of Germany. The second daughter joined the royal family of Holland, the third joined the royal family of some other country.

So all these royal families gathered recently upon the demise of the Greek queen. Vimalkirti's wife, Turiya, also went. Almost all of the European royal families are interwoven – someone's son or daughter is married into one royal family, then someone else's daughter is married into another royal family. In this way the Queen of Greece had power over almost all the royalty in Europe. Turiya told me that before her death, the queen had said, "No matter what happens, rescue Turiya and her daughter from the hands of Osho, because the shankaracharya has told me that there can be no more dangerous a man than him. This man is the enemy of religion."

And then there was a meeting of all the royalty of Europe that had attended the funeral of the queen in which it was decided that somehow or other my movement should be destroyed, that I should be destroyed somehow and that some clear plan of action should be drawn up to do this. Certainly with all of these people, either the kingdom is still in their hands... For example, Prince Philip: the whole effort was handed over to Prince Philip to create the strategy. And those who do not rule any more still have great power, still can have pressure over politicians, still have influence over the super rich.

If the parliaments of all the countries of Europe pass a law against me – that I cannot enter their countries – then the conspiracy is certainly international and the religious leaders, the politicians, the super rich are behind it. They have power.

But I want to make one thing clear: no matter how much power a lie may have, a lie is impotent in the face of truth. All those conspiracies will prove futile. If what I am saying is the truth and what I am doing is in tune with existence; if what I am saying belongs to eternal religiousness, then all conspiracies, all strategies will crumble. They have no value. That is why I do not try to deny them and waste my time either. They are lies that will die their own death.

I am the master of those whose hearts are rich with love. I am the master of those whose inner beings know the wealth of meditation. I am the master of those in whom the thirst for truth has arisen, the thirst to seek out the wealth of truth. If you want to call me "the rich man's guru," then I certainly am that – but then you will have to understand my definition of "the rich." Those who have got only lumps of gold and silver – I call them poor beggars. The rich man is one in whose heart there is peace, bliss, joy; in whose feet there is a dance and on whose breath there is a song. Only he within whom godliness has been glimpsed is rich. Those remaining are all poor.

Osho,
Why is this country not affluent in spite of forty years of
freedom, while in the same amount of time Russia, China and
Japan have turned into world powers? Can your philosophy
of life make India rich? Can you bring the paradise created
in Rajneeshpuram to the whole of India?

Certainly. There is no obstacle to India becoming rich except its ancient ideas. If some basic things can become clear in India's mind, it can become a world power within ten years.

The first thing to be understood is that there is no spirituality in poverty.

It is another matter if some rich man renounces his riches and becomes a beggar. But there will be a difference of earth and sky between this man's being a beggar and the beggarliness of the common beggar. This man's state of being a beggar is the next step after having known affluence, and the ordinary beggar has not yet had this experience. How can the common beggar reach to a step that can only occur after knowing wealth?

This false notion that poverty is spiritual has entered India's mind for a reason. It is because Buddha renounced his kingdom, Mahavira renounced his kingdom. Naturally logic says that when people walk away from wealth and become poor, become naked, then we poor are already blessed: we are already naked! There is no need to renounce anything nor to go anywhere. We do not need to renounce a kingdom or any wealth.

But you are mistaken. The dignity that is seen in Buddha could not have been there without him having renounced a kingdom. The experience of possessing a kingdom can be an experience of tremendous liberation in revealing that wealth is trivial, that nothing worthwhile can be achieved through it.

But the whole of India drew a wrong conclusion from this: that to remain poor is a worthy thing. After all what is the point when even emperors choose poverty? Then what is the point of renouncing poverty in the first place?

It is essential to erase the reverence for poverty from India's psyche.

It is essential to totally stop the population growth of India for thirty years.

For five years not a single child was born in Rajneeshpuram. There was no one forcing anything, there was nobody forcing anybody at a gunpoint. It is simply a matter of explaining and understanding: "With the amount of productive land we have, we cannot let the population grow beyond its limits." That is what the saying "getting too big for your blanket" means. Either the legs will be uncovered or the head; one or the other is bound to remain uncovered.

So for thirty years: no growth in India's population.

No emphasis should be given in India's universities, colleges and schools to the subjects that have no direct link with making today's life rich – for example, history, geography. Let technical knowledge, science, and meditation become the foundations of Indian education, and maintain a balance between these two: meditation should grow in the same proportions as science grows. If science grows and meditation does not, then there is a danger. Then it is like a naked sword coming into the hands of a child.

In India there are so many religions and they fight every day. This foolishness has to go. At least India should take the lead in the world that religion is one, and it has nothing to do with being a Hindu or with being a Mohammedan. It has to do with playing the music of one's inner being.

In the name of sannyas I have tried to spread that very religion, so that the energy that unnecessarily goes into fighting in India is used in creativity.

India's last forty years have gone to waste and there is a reason behind it. The first reason is that Mahatma Gandhi's vision was very primitive. It wasn't progressive, it stopped at the spinning wheel. We need to forget the spinning wheel, in fact we need to bury it – respectfully. Give respect to Gandhi because he worked tirelessly for this country's freedom, but it does not mean that the people who know how to fight for the country's freedom are also the people who know how to build the country. These are two separate things.

It is one thing to fight for the freedom of the country – that is a soldier's task, a warrior's task. All the members of my family went to jail during the freedom struggle. I used to ask them, "It's okay that the freedom you are fighting for is freedom from the British, but freedom for what? 'Freedom from' one can understand, but 'freedom for' what? What are you going to do once you have freedom?" I was small but I asked the great leaders of the country, I asked Jayaprakash Narayan: "If freedom comes today, what are you going to do? You don't have any plan or any clear-cut concept about what is to be done after the freedom."

And this became the biggest calamity. The same people who fought for freedom also became the rulers. They knew how to fight, but they did not know how to build, how to create. They had no relationship with that. They had never thought about it.

What is needed now is that we give the power to the hands of those people who are capable of infusing new creativity, a new vision of life and an opening up of new dimensions.

And there is no shortage of such people. If a scientist is born in India, he has to find a job in the West, because in the first place, there are no facilities, no modern labs in India for him to conduct experiments in. At the most he can become a professor but he won't be able to accomplish anything creative. If you want to build up India the emphasis has to be on creativity.

In the commune of five thousand people, there were scientists, there were surgeons, doctors, psychologists, psychiatrists; there were atomic physicists. And I can bring them all to India. There are no primitive, tribal people amongst my sannyasins. It is not a matter of Christian missionaries dealing with orphans and tribal people. Amongst my sannyasins are the world's most intelligent people. I can bring them all to India – all one million sannyasins – and I can put them into creative endeavors here in India.

But the government of this country wants to impose restrictions on me: that no sannyasin from outside can come to India. There is a limit to such foolishness! This government should know that we raise and educate our children, we send them to study in the West, and when they become ready after all the education and training, then the West absorbs them too. All the expenses are on us. The genius is ours but the West receives the final benefit. America knows how to draw all the genius from around the world.

Now I have that community of geniuses.

But this idiot government of ours – it is stopping my sannyasins from coming to India. It cannot stop them legally, so in the parliament the minister has said that we will not prevent sannyasins, but to the embassies messages are being sent not to allow my sannyasins to come. From everywhere sannyasins are sending me messages that they go to the Indian embassies and are told that there is no need for them to go to India.

A friend of mine recently informed me of this from Australia. I was shocked to hear that the Indian ambassador said to the young man, an engineer who is a sannyasin, "Why do you want to go to India?"

The young man said, "I want to go to India to learn meditation."

The Indian ambassador said, "India is no longer a place for learning meditation, yoga, etcetera. Those times are gone. Now we will not allow this kind of person to enter India."

These are our ambassadors! Somebody wants to come to India to learn meditation and our ambassador says, "Gone are those days. Now no one can go to India to learn meditation."

And for me, India is a symbol of nothing other than a place for learning meditation. It is a university of meditation, and not just today, but for centuries it has been a university of meditation.

Those forty years that we have lost can be reclaimed within ten years. But the only problem is that although fools die, they leave their offspring behind. And the old fools were better. Their offspring are a trouble beyond all imagination.

Osho,
Do you have a particular message that you would like
to give to Indians?

The only thing I want to say to India is: Recognize your real face. You are the country of Gautama the Buddha, and your ambassadors are saying that the doors are now closed for going to India for meditation. You are the country of Krishna, you are the country of Patanjali. You have given birth to stars that have no parallel in the world. All the stars of the whole sky are dim before your stars. Wake up, so that the petty politicians cannot exploit you and your coming generations; so that blind people do not lead a country of people with vision. Just remember, just remember all those fragrances again – the echoes of the Upanishads, the songs of Kabir, the dances of Meera. You are unparalleled.

Small people are ruling over you. Throw them off your chest! Your country is not yet devoid of intelligent people, but the intelligent people will not come to you begging for votes in the elections. Never vote for the one who comes begging for votes. Fall at the feet of someone whom you consider worthy of your vote. Persuade him to stand for the elections. "We want to vote for you."

The one who comes to you, begging for votes, is the small man. The one who has some value and some soul and some pride will not come begging from you. You will have to go to him and make your request.

India will have to provide the world with a new kind of democracy where the leader does not beg, where the people request the intelligent and sensible people for "a little of your time, a little of your intelligence – please give to this poor country too."

Osho defies categorization. His thousands of talks cover everything from the individual quest for meaning to the most urgent social and political issues facing society today. Osho's books are not written but are transcribed from audio and video recordings of his extemporaneous talks to international audiences. As he puts it, "So remember: whatever I am saying is not just for you... I am talking also for the future generations."

Osho has been described by *The Sunday Times* in London as one of the "1000 Makers of the 20th Century" and by American author Tom Robbins as "the most dangerous man since Jesus Christ." *Sunday Mid-Day* (India) has selected Osho as one of ten people – along with Gandhi, Nehru and Buddha – who have changed the destiny of India.

About his own work Osho has said that he is helping to create the conditions for the birth of a new kind of human being. He often characterizes this new human being as "Zorba the Buddha" – capable both of enjoying the earthy pleasures of a Zorba the Greek and the silent serenity of a Gautama the Buddha.

Running like a thread through all aspects of Osho's talks and meditations is a vision that encompasses both the timeless wisdom of all ages past and the highest potential of today's (and tomorrow's) science and technology.

Osho is known for his revolutionary contribution to the science of inner transformation, with an approach to meditation that acknowledges the accelerated pace of contemporary life. His unique OSHO Active Meditations™ are designed to first release the accumulated stresses of body and mind, so that it is then easier to take an experience of stillness and thought-free relaxation into daily life.

Two autobiographical works by the author are available:
Autobiography of a Spiritually Incorrect Mystic,
St Martins Press, New York (book and eBook)
Glimpses of a Golden Childhood,
OSHO Media International, Pune, India

Each year the Meditation Resort welcomes thousands of people from more than 100 countries. The unique campus provides an opportunity for a direct personal experience of a new way of living – with more awareness, relaxation, celebration and creativity. A great variety of around-the-clock and around-the-year program options are available. Doing nothing and just relaxing is one of them!

All programs are based on Osho's vision of "Zorba the Buddha" – a qualitatively new kind of human being who is able *both* to participate creatively in everyday life *and* to relax into silence and meditation.

Location
Located 100 miles southeast of Mumbai in the thriving modern city of Pune, India, the OSHO International Meditation Resort is a holiday destination with a difference. The Meditation Resort is spread over 28 acres of spectacular gardens in a beautiful tree-lined residential area.

OSHO Meditations
A full daily schedule of meditations for every type of person includes both traditional and revolutionary methods, and particularly the OSHO Active Meditations™. The meditations take place in what may be the world's largest meditation hall, the OSHO Auditorium.

OSHO Multiversity
Individual sessions, courses and workshops cover everything from

creative arts to holistic health, personal transformation, relationship and life transition, transforming meditation into a lifestyle for life and work, esoteric sciences, and the "Zen" approach to sports and recreation. The secret of the OSHO Multiversity's success lies in the fact that all its programs are combined with meditation, supporting the understanding that as human beings we are far more than the sum of our parts.

OSHO Basho Spa

The luxurious Basho Spa provides for leisurely open-air swimming surrounded by trees and tropical green. The uniquely styled, spacious Jacuzzi, the saunas, gym, tennis courts...all these are enhanced by their stunningly beautiful setting.

Cuisine

A variety of different eating areas serve delicious Western, Asian and Indian vegetarian food – most of it organically grown especially for the Meditation Resort. Breads and cakes are baked in the resort's own bakery.

Night life

There are many evening events to choose from – dancing being at the top of the list! Other activities include full-moon meditations beneath the stars, variety shows, music performances and meditations for daily life.

Or you can just enjoy meeting people at the Plaza Café, or walking in the nighttime serenity of the gardens of this fairytale environment.

Facilities

You can buy all your basic necessities and toiletries in the Galleria. The OSHO Multimedia Gallery sells a large range of OSHO media products. There is also a bank, a travel agency and a Cyber Café on-campus. For those who enjoy shopping, Pune provides all the options, ranging from traditional and ethnic Indian products to all of the global brand-name stores.

Accommodation

You can choose to stay in the elegant rooms of the OSHO Guest-house, or for longer stays on campus you can select one of the OSHO Living-In program packages. Additionally there is a plentiful variety of nearby hotels and serviced apartments.

www.osho.com/meditationresort
www.osho.com/guesthouse
www.osho.com/livingin

JAICO PUBLISHING HOUSE
Elevate Your Life. Transform Your World.

ESTABLISHED IN 1946, Jaico Publishing House is home to world-transforming authors such as Sri Sri Paramahansa Yogananda, Osho, The Dalai Lama, Sri Sri Ravi Shankar, Robin Sharma, Deepak Chopra, Jack Canfield, Eknath Easwaran, Devdutt Pattanaik, Khushwant Singh, John Maxwell, Brian Tracy and Stephen Hawking.

Our late founder Mr. Jaman Shah first established Jaico as a book distribution company. Sensing that independence was around the corner, he aptly named his company Jaico ('Jai' means victory in Hindi). In order to service the significant demand for affordable books in a developing nation, Mr. Shah initiated Jaico's own publications. Jaico was India's first publisher of paperback books in the English language.

While self-help, religion and philosophy, mind/body/spirit, and business titles form the cornerstone of our non-fiction list, we publish an exciting range of travel, current affairs, biography, and popular science books as well. Our renewed focus on popular fiction is evident in our new titles by a host of fresh young talent from India and abroad. Jaico's recently established Translations Division translates selected English content into nine regional languages.

Jaico's Higher Education Division (HED) is recognized for its student-friendly textbooks in Business Management and Engineering which are in use countrywide.

In addition to being a publisher and distributor of its own titles, Jaico is a major national distributor of books of leading international and Indian publishers. With its headquarters in Mumbai, Jaico has branches and sales offices in Ahmedabad, Bangalore, Bhopal, Bhubaneswar, Chennai, Delhi, Hyderabad, Kolkata and Lucknow.

SINCE 1946